UNIVERSITY OF NOTRE DAME
PUBLICATIONS IN MEDIAEVAL STUDIES
VOLUME XVIII

THE *DE GRAMMATICO* OF ST. ANSELM:

THE THEORY OF PARONYMY

PUBLICATIONS IN MEDIAEVAL STUDIES

THE UNIVERSITY OF NOTRE DAME

EDITOR: PHILIP S. MOORE, C.S.C.

ASSOCIATE EDITOR: JOSEPH N. GARVIN, C.S.C.

XVIII

The De Grammatico of
ST. ANSELM

THE THEORY
OF PARONYMY

BY DESMOND P. HENRY

UNIVERSITY OF MANCHESTER

UNIVERSITY OF NOTRE DAME PRESS 1964

PUBLICATIONS IN MEDIAEVAL STUDIES

I. The Works of Peter of Poitiers. *By Philip S. Moore.*
II. Commentarius Cantabrigiensis in Epistolas Pauli e schola Petri Abaelardi. *By Arthur Landgraf.*
  1. In Epistolam ad Romanos.
  2. In Epistolas ad Corinthios 1^{am} et 2^{am}, ad Galatos, et ad Ephesios.
  3. In Epistolas ad Philippenses, ad Colossenses, 1^{am} et 2^{am} ad Thessalonicenses, 1^{am} et 2^{am} ad Timotheum, ad Titum, et ad Philemonem.
  4. In Epistolam ad Hebraeos.
III. Petri Pictaviensis Allegoriae Super Tabernaculum Moysi. *By Philip S. Moore and James A. Corbett.*
IV. Johannis Dominici Lucula Noctis. *By Edmund Hunt.*
V. Sachsenspiegel and Bible. *By Guido Kisch.*
VI. Saint Bernward of Hildesheim. 1. His Life and Times. *By Francis J. Tschan.*
VII. Sententiae Petri Pictaviensis I. *By Philip S. Moore and Marthe Dulong.*
VIII. The 'Summulae logicales' of Peter of Spain. *By Joseph Patrick Mullally.*
IX. The Cyprus Passion Cycle. *By August C. Mahr.*
X. Pseudo–Philo's Liber Antiquitatum biblicarum. *By Guido Kisch.*
XI. Sententiae Petri Pictaviensis II. *By Philip S. Moore, Joseph N. Garvin, and Marthe Dulong.*
XII. Saint Bernward of Hildesheim. 2. His Works of Art. *By Francis J. Tschan.*
XIII. Saint Bernward of Hildesheim. 3. Album of All Extant Works. *By Francis J. Tschan.*
XIV. Student Life in Ave Maria College, Mediaeval Paris: History and Chartulary of the College. *By A. L. Gabriel.*
XV. Summa Contra Haereticos. *By Joseph N. Garvin and James A. Corbett.*
XVI. Navigatio sancti Brendani Abbatis. *By Carl Selmer.*
XVII. The Lineage of Lady Meed. The Development of Mediaeval Venality Satire. *By John A. Yunck.*
XVIII. The *De Grammatico* of St. Anselm. The Theory of Paronymy. *By Desmond P. Henry.*

In Preparation

Sententiae Petri Pictaviensis. III-V. *By P. S. Moore, J. N. Garvin, and M. Dulong.*
Stephani de Longuotona Cantuariensis archiepiscopi Quaestiones. *By J. N. Garvin.*
Aurora, Petri Rigae Canonis Rhemensis Biblia versificata. *By P. E. Beichner.*
Udonis Summa super Sententias Petri Lombardi. *By J. N. Garvin.*
The Summa "Breves dies hominis." *By J. N. Garvin.*

PREFACE

Recent serious work on the history of logic has tended to centre round syllogistic, propositional calculus, and extensions of the latter. Scarcely any advance has been made in the systematic study of those topics which form part of what the ancients would certainly have called "logic", yet which involve recourse to functors of semantical categories so complex, or so confused in current speech, that discussion of them has so far been in terms of "natural" language alone. The present work attempts not only to throw some light on part of what is, in effect, a complete blank in the history of logic, but also to exploit a manner in which the more neglected and supposedly more "informal" sectors of logical history may be brought under systematic control; the means suggested are those made available by recourse to part of the logic created by the Polish logician S. Leśniewski, namely, his Ontology. The philosophical and anti-formalist nature of this logic has recently been amply demonstrated in a work in the *Studies in Logic and the Foundations of Mathematics* series: "The Logical Systems of Leśniewski" by E. C. Luschei. Recourse to such a logic is a necessity which Saint Anselm would himself have recognized: in the absence of an adequate artificial language he had no alternative but to resort to nonsense in *De grammatico*. By such means the logician and philosopher are released from the necessity of merely regurgitating their historical subject-matter in terms of some present-day "natural" language which brings its own new modification to the original text and to the particular problems that go with it. There seems to be no reason why vast, neglected, and misunderstood areas of medieval logic and philosophy should not eventually be greatly clarified by recourse to means of the sort suggested.

I have to thank Dorothy M. Emmet for having kindly permitted me to undertake the present work. My chief immediate debt is to the works and conversation of Czeslaw Lejewski. The axiom, definitions, and theses of Ontology used in §6 were, for the most part, suggested to me by him; in particular, it is to him that I owe the definitions of the many-linked functors which are quite essential to the interpretations suggested; he also first identified such functors in the text itself. However, insofar as the details of the application of Ontology have been carried forward by me, he can in no way be held responsible for any errors which may have occurred in the course of my exposition. Others who have given me the benefit of their generous advice in immediate connection with the present project are A. N. Prior, Aelred Squire, O. P., W. C. Kneale, B. A. Wortley, J. M. Wallace-Hadrill, R. W. Southern, and D. M. Leahy.

The unfailing kindly interest of J. W. Harvey in my work and progress has been, and continues to be, a constant source of encouragement. Further, it was only on account of the teaching of A. M. MacIver that I was in the first place capable of in some measure appreciating the interest which *De grammatico* in particular, and Saint Anselm's work in general, might hold for the contemporary reader. To S. J. Curtis, whose lectures constituted my first systematic introduction to medieval thought my thanks are also due.

I have also to thank the publishers and editors mentioned below for their kind permission for the reproduction of the material indicated: the editors of ARCHIVUM LATINITATIS MEDII AEVI in T.XXVIII of which appeared my "Why 'Grammaticus'?" on which §4.1 and §4.2 are based; Gilbert Ryle, editor of MIND, in Vol. LXXII N.S. of which appeared my "Saint Anselm's Nonsense" on which §5 is based; B. Sobocinski, editor of NOTRE DAME JOURNAL OF FORMAL LOGIC, in Vol. III, No. 3 of which appeared my "An Anselmian Regress" on which §6.341 is based; Thomas Nelson and Sons Ltd. and F. S. Schmitt (Editor) whose text of *De grammatico* in S. ANSELMI OPERA OMNIA (Vol. I) constituted the point of departure for the version herein presented.

DESMOND PAUL HENRY

University of Manchester

REFERENCES

§0.1 *System of References*

§0.11 *Internal References.* The present study as a whole, including the text of the dialogue presented therein, has been broken down into numbered sections. Numbers referring to sections of the work apart from sections of the text of *De grammatico* are prefaced by "§" (e.g. §5.493); references to the dialogue's text (and hence also to the synopsis of that text (§2)), are each made by a number without any sign prefixed (e.g. 4.5022). As is evident from the examples given in the last sentence, the numbers in question each consist of two parts: that part before the decimal point refers to the main division; that part following the decimal point refers to a sub-division of the main division. Further, these numbers have in both cases been serially allocated in such a way that cross-references involving, say, only two digits, can be used as a global indication of all sections the left-hand digits of whose numbers are identical with the reference given: e.g. "§2.2" cross-refers to *all* sections, and their sub-paragraphs, which have numbers beginning as indicated; it hence refers to §2.201, §2.202, §2.21, §2.211, §2.212, and so on. The advantage of this use of decimals is that numbers can be allocated in such a way that they to some extent reflect the articulations (main heading, preliminary remarks, prime division, sub-division, sub-sub-division, and so on) of the theme or text to which reference is being made. In §6 inset sentences in the language of Ontology have been introduced, and are numbered serially within each minimal sub-division by means of a further decimal point followed by further digits; e.g. §6.22.11 refers to that sentence numbered ".11" in §6.22. Cross references within a minimal sub-division to sentences which it contains will not have the number of that sub-division prefixed, so that "§5.22.11" will not be used to refer to §5.22.11 within §5.22; instead, §5.22.11 will be referred to as ".11" within §5.22 only, and so on in similar cases.

§0.12 *External References*. Works to which reference is made will be indicated by the italicised *sigla* co-ordinated with their details which are given below. Generally, the *sigla* will be immediately followed by page or column numbers, as in "W35" and "B495". References to lines or groups of lines in works having their lines numbers will be made by adding a decimal point and the line number (e.g. "SNUW35.3") or the initial and terminal line-numbers of the groups (e.g. "A109.2.12"). Where works referred to are in several volumes, or are divided into books, the Roman numeral of the volume or book will immediately succeed the *siglum*, as in "SI 253.15.20". Anselm's works are not listed below, as their titles are usually quoted in full, and reference also made by means of "S". It should be noted that the numbers annexed to the references "APH" and "APA" are the numbers serially allotted to the paragraph divisions in the manual edition (Marietti). The references to *HSL* are by means of numbers having a decimal point on the same principle as the numbers used in the present work.

§0.13 *Sigla*:—

A	Abaelardus, Petrus	*Dialectica*	Ed. De Rijk
AC	Aristotle	*Categoriae*	
ADEE	Aquinas, Thomas	*De Ente et Essentia*	
ADI	Aristotle	*De Interpretatione*	
ADSE	Aristotle	*De Sophisticis Elenchis*	
AG3P	Anscombe-Geach	Three Philosophers	Blackwell 1961
AO	Abaelardus, Petrus	*Opera*	Ed. Cousin 1859
AP	Aristotle	*Analytica Priora*	
APA	Aquinas, Thomas	Comm. on Post. Analytics	Ed. Spiazzi 1955
APH	Aquinas, Thomas	Comm. on Peri Hermeneias	Ed. Spiazzi 1955
ASCG	Aquinas, Thomas	*Summa Contra Gentiles*	
AST	Aquinas, Thomas	*Summa Theologica*	
B	Boethius	*Opera Omnia (Tomus Posterior)*	PL 64
BC	Boethius	*In Categorias Aristotelis*	B159 - B294

BCP	Boethius	*Commentaria in Porphyrium*	*B*71 - *B*158
BD	Boethius	*Liber de Divisione*	*B*875 - *B*892
BDF	Boethius	*Liber de Definitione*	*B*891 - *B*910
BDIG	Boethius	Greater commentary on *ADI*	*B*393 - *B*640
BDIL	Boethius	Lesser commentary on *ADI*	*B*293 - *B*392
BDP	Boethius	*Dialogi in Porphyrium*	*B*9 - *B*70
BDT	Boethius	*De Differentiis Topicis*	*B*1173 - *B*1216
BSH	Boethius	*De Syllogismo Hypothetico*	*B*831 - *B*876
BTC	Boethius	*Comm. in Topica Ciceronis*	*B*1039 - *B*1174
CR	Church, A.	Review (J. of Symbolic Logic)	Vol. 8 (1943) p.46
CIA	Cousin, V.	*Ouvrages Inédits d'Abélard*	Paris 1836
GPMA	Gilson, E.	*La Philosophie au Moyen Age*	Payot 1944
HA	Henry, D. P.	Saint Anselm's Nonsense	*Mind* Jan. 1963
HG	Henry, D. P.	The *De grammatico* of S. Anselm	*Philosophical Quarterly* Vol. 10, No. 39, 1960
HH	Hauréau, B.	*Hist. de la Philosophie Scolastique, Première Partie*	Paris 1872
HL	Henry, D. P.	The Scope of the Logic of St. Anselm	*L'homme et son destin* (Louvain 1960)
HM	Henry, D. P.	Remarks on St. Anselm's treatment of Possibility	*Spicilegium Beccense* I (Paris 1959)
HN	Henry, D. P.	Numerically Definite Reasoning in the *Cur Deus Homo*	Dominican Studies Vol. VI
HP	Henry, D. P.	The *Proslogion* Proofs	*Philosophical Quarterly* Vol. 5, 1955
HSL	Hispanus, Petrus	*Summulae Logicales*	Ed. Bochenski 1947

HSP	Hunt, R. W.	Studies on Priscian in the 11th and 12th Centuries	Medl. and Renaissance Studies, Vol. I, No. 2
HW	Henry, D. P.	Why *"Grammaticus"*?	*Archivum Latinitatis Medii Aevi* T. XXVIII
JL	Joseph, H. W. B.	An Introduction to Logic	2nd Edn. 1916
K	Keil, H.	*Grammatici Latini*	Leipzig
KF	Kapp, E.	Greek Foundations of Traditional Logic	Columbia U. P. 1942
KSE	Keynes, J. W.	Studies and Exercises in Formal Logic	3rd. Edn. 1894
LA	Lejewski, C.	Proper Names	Aristotelian Soc. Supp. Vol. XXXI
LLE	Lejewski, C.	Logic and Existence	Brit. J. for the Philosophy of Science, 1954
LP		The Port-Royal Logic	Tr. T. S. Baynes
LR	Lejewski, C.	On Leśniewski's Ontology	*Ratio* Vol. I, 1958
LTD	Lejewski, C.	A re-examination of the Russellian Theory of Descriptions	*Philosophy,* Vol. XXXV No. 132, 1960
MC	McCabe, H.	Categories	*Dominican Studies* Vol. VII
MD	MacIver, A. M.	Demonstratives and Proper Names	*Philosophy and Analysis* pp. 26 - 32
MID	Minto, W.	Logic Inductive and Deductive	London 1894
MMP	Maurice, F. D.	Medieval Philosophy	London 1857
MP	Macdonald, Margaret	The Philosopher's use of Analogy	Proc. Arist. Soc. 1937-8
MSL	Mill, J. S.	System of Logic	5th Edn. 1862
OPW	Ockham, W.	Philosophical Writings	Ed. Boehner, 1957
PBT	Paré, Brunet and Tremblay	*La Renaissance du XII° siècle*	Vrin, 1933
PFL	Prior, A. N.	Formal Logic	Oxford, 1955, 1962
PG	Prantl, C.	*Geschichte der Logik im Abendlande*	Vol. II, 1861

PH	Prete, S.	*"Humanus" nella letteratura arcaica latina*	Marzorati 1948
PL		*Patrologia Latina*	Ed. J. P. Migne
Q	Quine, W. V. O.	From a Logical Point of View	Harvard 1953
RI	Russell, B.	Intro. to Mathematical Philosophy	London 1919

CONTENTS

THE *DE GRAMMATICO* OF ST. ANSELM:

THE THEORY OF PARONYMY

I

INTRODUCTION

§1.01   The present introduction contains a brief résumé of past misunderstandings of St. Anselm's dialogue *De grammatico*. Readers who primarily desire an informal account of the way in which the dialogue may be brought within the ambit of contemporary logical discussion need only consult §5; the latter is enlarged on by recourse to a modern logical language in §6. Historical affiliations of the theme are outlined in §4.

§1.1   Few logical works can have been so forcefully condemned as has the dialogue *De grammatico*. Written by St. Anselm of Canterbury about nine hundred years ago, it has received scant notice from the more sympathetic critics, while the less sympathetic have been most severe. One of the aims of this study is to suggest that the charges so often directed against it are quite unfounded, and at the same time to draw attention to its undoubedly positive value.

§1.2   The dialogue was composed during Anselm's period at the monastery of Bec, in Normandy, which he entered in the year one thousand and sixty, and of which he became Prior in one thousand and seventy-eight. It is mentioned in the preface to his

De Veritate as being one of a group of four dialogues; three of these, he declares, deal with scriptural matters, while the fourth, *De grammatico*, can be employed as an aid in the introductory study of logical argument. Yet in spite of this avowal of the dialogue's elementary level, it is a most remarkable and mysterious fact that no two histories of thought appear agreed as to the precise nature of its topic. According to Cousin its cardinal point is a difficulty arising from Aristotle's *De Interpretatione* (*CIA* ciii); more recent authors see it as an exercise in Aristotelian categorisation (*PBT*199); Maurice believes that it concerns the question, "Whether a Grammarian is a Substance or a Quality" (*MMP*110); for Hauréau it is an exercise in the profane art of logic, which Anselm finds pleasant, and yet which has nothing at all in common with his theological works (*HH*268). All are agreed, however, that we are here faced with a trivial school matter. The more tolerant critics condescend to excuse this triviality (*PBT*199), whereas others see the whole thing as a typical piece of scholastic barbarism. There is likewise unanimity as to the contrast which holds between this work and Anselm's other writings (*CIA*ciii, *MMP*110). Prantl parrots Cousin's judgement of the work, condemns it as futile, wandering, tiresome, and laborious, grossly misunderstands it, and even goes so far as to propose "corrections" to the text in order to bring it into line with his misunderstandings (*PG*II 93, n.363). Maurice's remarks serve to bring out another quite extraordinary point, namely that the dialogue's title, which is taken from its *incipit*, has never been satisfactorily translated into any West European language; his interpretation of *Dialogus de grammatico* as "Dialogue on the Grammarian" commits him to a totally false impression of its theme. Most commentators seem to have realized dimly that there is some difficulty here, and have hence tended to retain the Latin title. The reasons, philological and logical, for this state of affairs are in fact quite complex, and are explained in §4.2 and §5.31.

§1.3   It must be admitted, however, that the dialogue is not easy to follow; semantical categories not usually encountered or recognised in pre-theoretical speech are used, yielding sentences which Anselm admits are nonsense from the point of view of ordinary speech. Maurice's account is hence a fair representation of the bafflement which would still be experienced by a modern reader. Again, Anselm erects a logical structure in which every word, every phrase, and every example, have their place, point, and complex historical background; in the absence of any system of minute cross-reference and comment, however, little of this is apparent at first sight. The text of the dialogue here presented has hence been subjected to detailed division and numeration in order to facilitate cross-reference. At the same time a synopsis incorporating that numeration has been provided so as to enable the larger articulations of the work to be more easily perceived. Only by means of such expositions and aids can something like the true significance of each proposition, and of the whole, be brought into relief; when one knows the origin of the various topics, their development in Anselm's other works and at the hands of his predecessors and successors, as well as their bearing in terms of the fine co-ordinates made available by the logic of Leśniewski (§6), then, and perhaps only then, can anything approaching a true understanding be attained. This applies not only to *De grammatico* and the rest of Anselm's works, but also to the philosophical and logical aspects of medieval writings in general. Worse than useless is the attempt to read them without some realisation of these facts.

§1.4   The interest of *De grammatico* can nevertheless be shown to extend far beyond the bounds of mere literary curiosity and the *minutiae* of the history of logic; the theory of meaning which emerges from it has several links with the subtleties of modern logical theory, as will become apparent in §5 and §6. This will doubtless still not serve to shake the prejudices of people who know nothing about the history of philosophy in the two thousand years between Plato and Descartes, and who, taking advantage of the "Enlightenment" and of the positivist short-cuts to avoid the bother of doing history, especially the history of thought, allow themselves to vaticinate from an *a priori* rag-bag of odds and ends on all the horrid goings-on of that two thousand years, including the crude theories of meaning which, as is sometimes supposed, imprisoned European thought during that period.

II

SYNOPSIS OF *DE GRAMMATICO*

§2.1   The numbered divisions into which the text of the dialogue has, in §3, been broken down, are of course reproduced in the synopsis of that text which now follows. The letters "S" and "T" have, for the purposes of this synposis only, been prefixed to the textual numbers in order to indicate which of the two interlocutors of the dialogue, Student or Tutor respectively, is responsible for the material so numbered.

§2.2   Although the numbered divisions of the dialogue are intended to reflect somewhat the articulations of the text, as well as for convenience in cross-reference, the numeration makes no universal claim to that degree of *finesse* which would enable the comparative importance of the various assertions to be gauged accurately. At certain points the division of the material has been carried slightly further in the synopsis; where this has occurred, the additional reference-numbers resulting are enclosed in square brackets. For the purpose of symmetrical presentation it has also been considered helpful to reverse the order of certain syllogistic premisses; e.g. 3.5332 appears before 3.5331 in this synopsis, but not, of course, in the text.

§2.30   As the synopsis is presented in English, some remarks which apply also to the translation suggested in §3 may be added at this point. The text of the dialogue was written in eleventh-century Latin which contained neither quotation-marks nor articles, definite or indefinite, and a modern reproduction and translation of that text might at least appear to demand the introduction of clarificatory quotation-marks; articles are certainly needed to produce recognisable English sentences for the translation. However, as §5 and §6 will reveal, the discourse at times moves in terms of, and is intended to draw attention to, novel semantical categories not recognised by ordinary grammar; there is therefore a temptation to use articles and quotation marks in order to minimise the oddness of certain assertions involving such categories. In point of fact such a minimisation of oddness would certainly result in a failure to reproduce the point of the original; in some cases the use of quotation marks or the selection of one or other of the assortment of sensible sentences which the addition of the various possible English articles would permit in translation would issue in a straight contradiction of Anselm's intentions. In order to avoid the one-sided and sometimes misleading options to which the use of quotation marks and articles would thus commit one, the text as reproduced contains no quotation marks, and the translation encloses in quotation marks only those sentences which are clearly in course of being mentioned by the interlocutors; elsewhere italicisation has been resorted to in order to indicate *either* the mention of a word or words *or* the use of a word in a way that involves novel semantical categories appropriate to the technical discussion in progress. Finally, articles, both indefinite and definite, have been placed in brackets at those points in the translation where their occurrence in technical assertions might conceivably constitute a restrictive prejudice or a diversion from the intention of the original. Such devices to some extent obviate the temptation to embark on unnecessary discussions centred round the idiosyncrasies of the English language. The policy outlined appears to exhaust the resources of natural language, as usually printed, for making clear the intentions of Anselm; to go any further an artificial language of the sort introduced in §6 is called for.

§2.31 The difficulty about finding a consistent translation for "*grammaticus*" is, when compared with the issues raised in the last paragraph, a perfectly familiar difficulty, and will be dealt with at length in §4.2.

§2.32 At various points in the dialogue there occur phrases which are intended to be equivalents of a single shared name; examples of such phrases are, "*qui habet essentiam grammatici*" (for "*grammaticus*") and "*qui habet albedinem*" (for "*albus*"). One would normally be inclined to render the "*qui*" of such phrases in translation as "he who", yielding "he who has the essence of literate" and "he who has whiteness" respectively. At once it is apparent, from a logical point of view, that interpretation in this fashion constitutes a restriction on the range of application appropriate to the names whose meanings (or equivalents) are thus interpreted: this restriction is to persons, as opposed to impersonal or personal objects of any kind. The question hence arises: to what extent is the adoption of such restriction-imposing translation justified in the present context? Anselm's having chosen (as is customary when dealing with questions of meaning, lexicography, or allied studies) the nominative masculine form of these adjectives, has left him no choice in the form which sentences stating or relying on such equations may take; given the Latin grammar within whose framework he is working, "*qui*" and only "*qui*" is appropriate. At one point he is plainly striving for full generality, for a form of expression which commits the user to no restrictions as to the nature (person or thing) of that to which the adjective applies, and hence uses both neuter and masculine forms of the adjective: *in hac domo est* album *sive* albus; *an scis per hoc ibi esse equum?* . . . *Non* . . . (4.421). This kind of striving, and the nature of the whole topic of the dialogue, with its distinction between pure meaning and factual application, already suggest that the restrictions normally imposed on the translator by the use of "*qui*" in such phrases as the ones quoted need not be adhered to in the present case; "*qui*" could thus be rendered "that which", as opposed to the *prima facie* "he who". This possibility is reinforced when some of the doctrines of the dialogue are considered in more detail. Thus, given the thesis the "literate" *("grammaticus")*

no more signifies man than does "white" *("albus")* (4.24121) it is
plain that restriction to "he who" in the elucidation of the signification of these two words would in fact be a betrayal of Anselm's intentions, since this would imply that only persons (as opposed to
mere things) were comprised in their meaning. That the import of
"albus" is supposed to be completely unrestricted to the personal is
also shown by the Student's contention that the word does not
signify any determinate haver of whiteness — not even a physical
object of some kind — it just signifies an *indeterminate something*
which has whiteness: *albus cum sit idem quod habens albedinem,
non significat determinate hoc vel illud habens, velut corpus, sed
indeterminate aliquid habens albedinem* (4.801). Even this inde-
terminacy fails to satisfy the Tutor — even the "indeterminate something" must be expelled from the meaning of *"albus"* (4.811). Under
circumstances such as these, it would be a plain betrayal of Anselm's
thesis to insist that the *"qui"* of *"albus est qui habet albedinem"* (and
sentences or phrases stating or relying upon a like equation) should
be translated as "he who" or in any way which entails restrictions
to persons as the referents of the words. Accordingly *"qui"* has in
such context been translated as "that which" throughout the version
which is offered, and in the synopsis which now follows.

SYNOPSIS

S1.000   *Introduction.* What account is to be given of things named
         paronymously? For example, given that *literate* is a par-
         onym, which of the following is true?

[S1.001]   *literate* is [a] substance
[S1.002]   *literate* is [a] quality

S1.100   On the one hand, that
S1.101   *literate* is [a] substance   1.001
         can be proved, since the following are true:
S1.11   Every literate is [a] man

S1.12   Every man is [a] substance

S1.13   For [a] literate's being [a] man [1.11] is the only condition of its being such that its substantiality ensues. Hence, it being granted that [a] literate is [a] man, the same things follow from *literate* as from *man*.

S1.20   On the other hand, philosophers' treatises contain the assertion that

S1.201   *literate* is [a] quality   1.002

S1.21   And these alternatives [1.001, 1.002] are mutually incompatible.

T2.00   Both alternatives [1.001, 1.002] are valid, and the task is to show how they are not incompatible.

3.0   *First discussion of* 1.11
S3.100   First disproof of 1.11:
S3.101   No literate can be understood without literacy
S3.102   Every man can be understood without literacy
[3.103   Hence: No literate is [a] man]
S3.110   Second disproof of 1.11:
S3.111   Every literate is susceptible of degree
S3.112   No man is susceptible of degree
S3.113   Hence: No literate is [a] man.

T3.20   Refutation of 3.10, 3.11, by absurd conclusions from proof of same form:
T3.21   *Animal* may be defined as *animated sensitive substance,* so that
T3.221   Every animal can be understood without rationality
T3.222   No man can be understood without rationality
[3.223   Hence: No man is animal.]

T3.231   Further: No animal is necessarily rational
T3.232   Every man is necessarily rational
T3.233   Hence: No man is animal.
S3.234   In 3.22, 3.23, a false conclusion is derived from true premises by means of valid argument-forms similar to those of 3.10, 3.11. This indicates the necessity for analysis.

T3.30   *Analysis of* 3.10, 3.11:

T3.310   First analysis of 3.10:

T3.311   3.102 = Every man can be understood to be man without literacy

T3.312   3.101 = No literate can be understood to be literate without literacy.

T3.3121   The two premises 3.102 and 3.101 as now analysed are shown to have no common term, and hence are incapable of producing a conclusion according to the rules of syllogism.

S3.320   Analysis of 3.11 by a method similar to that of 3.31 yields:

S3.321   3.112 = No man is susceptible of degree as man

S3.322   3.111 = Every literate is susceptible of degree as literate.

S3.3221   So that the premises 3.112, 3.111, as now analysed are shown to have no common term, and hence are incapable of producing a conclusion according to the rules of syllogism.

T3.33   The capacity of premises to produce a conclusion by means of a middle term should be decided rather by analysis of the meanings involved than by attention to the standard lay-out of terms in accordance with syllogistic rules.

T3.40   Hence are possible second versions of 3.311, 3.322, which show that 3.10 was not altogether misguided:

T3.41   3.311 = Being [a] man does not require literacy

T3.42   3.312 = Being [a] literate requires literacy.

T3.430   Hence, by means of the common term now revealed, one can infer:

T3.431   Being [a] literate is not being [a] man

T3.44   i.e. *literate* and *man* are not identically defined.

T3.450   However, from 3.431 it does not follow that

T3.451   [a] literate is not [a] man   [3.103, 3.113]
           but only

T3.452   [a] literate is not the same as [a] man
           in the sense of 3.44

T3.500   Test question: how can the following be refuted?

T3.501   Every literate is asserted [to be] so in respect of quality

T3.502   No man is asserted [to be] so in respect of quality

T3.503   Hence: no man is literate.

S3.510   Imitation of method of 3.2 to refute 3.50; the latter is like:

S3.511   Every rational is asserted [to be] so in respect of quality

S3.512   No man is asserted [to be] so in respect of quality

S3.513   Hence: No man is rational (or: *Rational* is predicated of no man).

S3.520   Imitation of the method of 3.31 to refute 3.50; the latter is analysable thus:

S3.521   3.501 = Every literate is asserted [to be] literate in respect of quality

S3.5220   3.502 = No man is asserted [to be] man in respect of quality.

S3.5221   But from these two true premisses it cannot be concluded that *literate* is predicated of no man (cf.3.503), since they now have no common term.

S3.530   But the inference would become a valid one, because of the existence of a common term, were the major premiss (3.521) to remain as before (3.531) and the new minor premiss shown below (3.532) to become true, thus:

S3.531   Every literate is asserted [to be] literate in respect of quality (3.521)

S3.532   No man is asserted [to be] literate in respect of quality

[3.5321   Hence: *literate* is not predicated of any man.]

S3.5330   Alternatively, a common term would ensue were the minor premiss (3.522) to remain as before (3.5331) and the new major premiss shown below (3.5332) to become true, thus:

S3.5332   Every literate is asserted [to be] man in respect of quality

S3.5331   No man is asserted [to be] man in respect of quality

S3.5333   Hence: *literate* is not predicated of any man.

S3.540   And if the assertion "[a] man is not [a] literate" (cf.3.451) is understood to assert the non-identity of *man* and *literate* (cf.3.542) then from the premises in question here (3.501, 3.502) it does follow that

S3.541   No man is literate (3.503)

S3.542   since what is in a certain sense a common term (cf. 3.53) has been shown to emerge, and this is at least sufficient to prove that

S3.543   The essence of [a] man is not the essence of [a] literate.

T3.60   Reply to 3.5: The argument of 3.5 will not do. It contains, among other faults, a misguided imitation of 3.31, 3.4. Hence a further analysis of 3.10 now follows.

T3.610   Consider a case apparently similar to 3.10:

T3.611   No man can be understood without rationality

T3.612   Every stone can be understood without rationality

T3.6121   Hence: No stone is [a] man.

T3.620   Now 3.6121 means

T3.621   [a] stone is *in no sense* [a] man
and not just

T3.622   [a] stone is not the same as [a] man.

T3.630   How then do 3.611, 3.612 differ from 3.101, 3.102?

S3.631   By the method of 3.31 a refutation of 3.61 would consist in showing its premises to contain no common term, thus:

S3.6311   3.611 [=] a man cannot be understood to be [a] man without rationality

S3.6312   3.612 [=] a stone cannot be understood to be [a] stone without rationality.

S3.6313   But in fact the strong form (3.621) of the conclusion (3.6121) of 3.61 is true. If 3.61 cannot withstand this analysis, how then can 3.10?

T3.6320   The point of introducing 3.61 is that 3.61 and 3.10 are *not* really similar cases, for 3.61 can be analysed thus:

T3.6321   3.611 = No man is in some sense understandable without rationality

T3.6322   3.612 = Every stone is in any sense understandable without rationality

T3.63221 Hence: No stone is in any sense [a] man (cf. 3.621).

T3.6330 Whereas 3.10 cannot be similarly analysed as:

T3.6331 3.101 = No literate is in some sense understandable without literacy

T3.6332 3.102 = Every man is in any sense understandable without literacy

For on the contrary, it is the case that:

T3.6333 Every thing which is literate can be understood to be [a] man without literacy

T3.6334 No man can be understood to be [a] literate without literacy.

T3.6340 Hence is shown the dissimilarity between 3.611, 3.612 (cf. 3.632) and 3.101, 3.102; for in view of 3.633, the premisses 3.101, 3.102 cannot have as their conclusion:

T3.6341 [a] literate is in no sense [a] man.

S3.700 Objection to the analysis of 3.10 given at 3.4:

S3.701 If being [a] literate is not being [a] man (3.431) then whatever is essentially literate need not therefore be essentially man.

However,

S3.71 If *man* follows from *literate*, then the essence of *man* follows from the essence of *literate*.

S3.711 But, by 3.701 and 3.431, the consequent consequence of 3.71 is false, hence also the antecedent one, so that

S3.7111 Not every literate is [a] man.

S3.720 Now either every literate is [a] man, or none are,

S3.721 But 3.7111 falsifies the first of these alternatives, hence

S3.7211 No literate is [a] man.

T3.800 Indirect refutation of 3.7 by outline of absurd conclusion from proof of the same form:

T3.8010 If both *man* and *animal* are definable as *rational mortal animal*, then there is a universal identity of objects to which *rational mortal* and *animal* apply.

T3.8011 But the consequent of 3.8010 is false.

T3.8012 Hence also its antecedent is false, i.e. being [a] man is not being [an] animal (cf. 3.431, 3.44).

T3.810   Now use of 3.8012 in the same way as 3.431 is used in 3.7 would give the absurd conclusion:

T3.811   No man is [an] animal.

T3.900   Direct refutation of 3.7:

T3.901   3.431 = 3.44 = [a] literate and [a] man are not altogether identical; (cf. 3.41, 3.42, 3.452).

T3.910   Hence 3.701 should read:

T3.911   If being literate is not being [a] man and only [a] man, then whatsoever is essentially literate need not on that account be essentially man and only man.

T3.920   It follows that when 3.71 has its antecedent consequence negated (cf. 3.711), but now in accordance with 3.901, that negation should read:

T3.921   *man* and only *man* does not follow from *literate*

T3.922   i.e. if something is literate it does not follow that it is [a] man and only [a] man.

T3.930   Hence the only conclusion from 3.7 is:

T3.931   No literate is [a] man and only [a] man.

T3.940   If it can be shown that

T3.9410   Being [a] literate is not being [a] man is like

T3.9411   Being [a] white is not being [a] man,

the sense of the latter being:

T3.9412   [a] man can be without [a] white, and [a] white can be without [a] man,

T3.9420   then from 3.941 it follows that

T3.9421   Some literate can be other than [a] man.

T3.9430   Nevertheless it is now clear that

T3.9431   There is some non-human literate

cannot be shown.

4.0   *Second discussion of* 1.11

S4.100   Second disproof of 1.11:

S4.101   [a] literate is in a subject

S4.102   No man is in a subject

S4.103   Hence: No literate is [a] man.

T4.1100 This argument (4.10) involves (in 4.101) a consequence improperly drawn from Aristotle.

T4.1101 When the word *literate* is being used in talk about a literate, then it can be agreed that:

T4.1102   When *literate* is heard, then *man* or literacy is understood, and

T4.1103   When [a] literate is being talked about, the talk is either about [a] man or about literacy.

T4.1104 Now [a] man is [a] substance, and not in a subject,

T4.1105 And literacy is [a] quality, and is in a subject.

   Under these circumstances (4.110) one might say that

T4.111   [a] literate is [a] substance and not in a subject (cf. 3.101) insofar as man is concerned (cf. 4.102), and

T4.112   *literate* is [a] quality and is in a subject (cf. 4.101) insofar as literacy is concerned.

S4.1200 Objections to 4.111:

S4.1201 *Literate* is neither a primary nor a secondary substance, since

S4.121 *Literate* is in a subject, is asserted of many things, and is therefore not primary substance, and

S4.122 *Literate* is neither genus nor species nor is it asserted in respect of "whatness", and is therefore not secondary substance.

T4.130 Reply to 4.12:

T4.131 Against 4.122: insofar as a literate being is not in a subject, it falls under both genus and species (*animal* and *man*) and to this extent is secondary substance and is asserted in respect of whatness.

T4.132 Against 4.121: insofar as a certain literate being is not in a subject, it is individual and is therefore primary substance.

T4.14 Has it not now been shown that (i) *literate* can be used in speech to refer to man (cf. 4.1103, 4.111) and is in this respect a substance, and (ii) its cognitive content is *literacy,* and it is in this respect a quality (cf. 1.00)?

S4.20   How can it be said that *literate* signifies a quality (i.e. literacy)? After all, if one tries to use the word to refer to literacy, then nonsense results.

S4.210   And there is a glaring discrepancy between the assertions involving *literate* which logicians make in their writings, and their use of the word in everyday talk.

S4.211   For they often give *literate* as an example of a word signifying a quality or an accident,

S4.212   Whereas everyone's current manner of utterance shows that *literate* is a substance (man) rather than a quality (literacy) (cf. 4.210).

S4.22   The crux of the matter is this: if we are to say that *literate* is [a] quality as well as [a] substance, why should not the same be said of *man?*

T4.230   Substance-signifying words (e.g. *man*) and paronyms (e.g. *literate*) signify in very dissimilar fashions.

T4.231   Thus *man* signifies principally substance—the unitary completion of the incomplete.

T4.232   Whereas of *literate* one can say that it signifies literacy (a quality) precisively, and *man* (a substance) only obliquely.

T4.233   *Literate* is, however, appellative (cf. 4.2341) of *man*, but does not signify (properly or precisively) *man.*

T4.2340   *Literate* in fact signifies precisively literacy, without at the same time being appellative of literacy.

T4.2341   And a name is *appellative* of that to which it is used to refer in the current course of utterance, as opposed to that to which logical assertions may make it appear to refer (cf. 4.20, 4.21). And certainly, in ordinary talk as opposed to logical talk (cf. 4.5022) one does not say that *literate* is literacy, but that a literate is a man.

S4.2400   *Objection*: is not *literate* definable as *man displaying literacy?* How can this be reconciled with 4.233, 4.234?

T4.2410   Five arguments against the definition proposed in 4.2400:

T4.2411 (1) If literate is defined as *man displaying literacy,* i.e. if literacy becomes a constitutive characteristic, then logic is disorganized.

T4.24120 (2) A non-human literate can at least be supposed, hence a possible contradiction can be inferred if the definition of 4.2400 is adhered to.

T4.24121 Hence also, *literate* no more signifies *man* than *white* does (cf. 3.941). It just happens to be the case that man alone has literacy (cf. 4.51), but is not the only haver of whiteness.

T4.2413 (3) The assertion *Socrates is an animal man* is inapt because *animal* is already understood when *man* is used; but *Socrates is a literate man* is quite apt, hence *literate* does not include *man.*

T4.2414 (4) Iterated substitutions effected in *Socrates is a literate man* according to the definition of 4.2400, and the equation of *man displaying literacy* with *literate man,* lead to infinite regress.

T4.2415 (5) Generalisation of the synonymy proposed in 4.2400 in respect of all paronyms will alter the classification of the paronym *today's* as a part of speech.

T4.30 Thus is confirmed the doctrine of 4.232, 4.233, namely that *literate* does not, strictly speaking, signify *man.*

T4.31 And the sense in which *literate* signifies *literacy* may be seen by subducting *man* from the phrase suggested as synonymous in 4.240, so as to truncate it to . . . *displaying literacy;* (cf. 4.8).

S4.40 Further difficulties arising from 4.23:

S4.411 *Literate* is not appellative of literacy (4.234) but of man (4.233).

S4.412 *Literate* is not significative of *man* (4.233) but of literacy (4.234).

S4.413 Yet *literate* is significative of both literacy (precisively) (4.234) and of man (obliquely), and hence arise the paradoxes:

S4.414   *Literate* is not significative of *man* (4.412) and yet is (4.413).

S4.415   *Literate* is appellative of man (4.411) yet is not significative of man (4.412).

T4.420   Reply to 4.4: clarification of terminology by example:

T4.4210   The assertion "[a] white is within this building", spoken in respect of an enclosed white horse of which the hearer knows nothing, conveys to the hearer no reference to a horse.

S4.4211   And although the assertion may arouse the empirically-grounded expectation of a body or surface which has the whiteness, yet this expectation reflects something other than the precisive signification.

T4.422   In contrast, the command, "Strike [the] white!", when addressed to a hearer confronted with a black bull and a white horse, would convey that the horse was in question, even though the word *horse* is not actually used.

T4.4231   The word *horse* signifies [the] horse precisively, not obliquely.

T4.4232   The word *white* signifies [the] horse obliquely, *via* the context of utterance, and not precisively.

T4.4233   The word *white* signifies the phrase . . . *having whiteness*, and a similar lack of completeness is found in the cognitive content conveyed by the word.

T4.4234   This incompleteness is remedied by means of sense-acquaintance with the context of utterance, e.g. by seeing that the whiteness is that of the horse. The word *white* of itself only signifies the horse obliquely, by means of that sense-acquaintance. Nevertheless, *white* is in this case appellative of the horse.

S4.4240   Thus are solved the difficulties of 4.41:

S4.4241   The paronym *white* signifies [a] substance not precisively, but obliquely, and is appellative of substance.

S4.4242   This finding can be extended in like manner to all paronyms.

S4.4243 The distinction between precisive and oblique signification can also be extended to verbs as well as to names.

T4.430 Precisive signification pertains essentially to significant
utterances as such; oblique signification is only accident-
ally linked with such utterances (cf. 4.515).

T4.431 When parts of speech are defined as *significant utterances,*
precisive signification is then in question (cf. 4.2415).

S4.500 Supposed difficulties following from the proof (4.24,
4.3) that *literate* signifies literacy alone, and not *man*
and literacy:

S4.501 How can [a] literate be [a] quality (literacy)?

S4.5020 How can man alone, i.e. without literacy, be literate?

S4.5021 For either man alone is literate or man along with literacy
is literate; but by 4.3 it is false that *man* and *literacy* are
literate, hence man alone is literate (cf. 4.24121).

S4.5022 And (cf. 4.501) the answer to the question "what is [a]
literate?" can scarcely be "*Literate* is *literacy*"or "*Literate*
is a quality".

S4.503 Further, to be [a] literate [a] man must have literacy, i.e.
must not be man alone.

T4.510 Reply to 4.502: the word *alone* in "Man alone is literate"
can have two senses:

T4.511 Correct sense: "Man alone ever possesses literacy (and
nothing else ever does possess literacy)".

T4.5120 Incorrect sense: "Man alone (deprived of literacy) is literate".

T4.5121 The correct sense (4.511) corresponds to the case of the
first member of a linearly ordered couple (e.g. a leader):
that first member *alone* precedes. The incorrect sense
(4.5120) corresponds to the case of that which is *alone,*
and hence cannot precede anything else.

T4.5122 Reply to 4.501: The assertion "Literate is [a] quality"
must be understood according to the special usage of
Aristotle's *Categoriae.*

S4.513   But it would seem to follow from the *Categoriae* that [a]
           literate is [a] substance, since man alone is literate.

T4.5141   Aristotle's main intention in that treatise was to deal with
           the signification of words, not the categorisation of things.

T4.5142   He was not primarily concerned with the natures of things,
           nor with the things of which words happen to be appel-
           lative, but with what the words signify.

T4.5143   This involved, however, assertions in terms of things.

T4.5144   His turn of expression at the opening of the *Categoriae*
           proves that 4.5142 is the case.

T4.515   Aristotle in fact dealt with words insofar as they are essen-
           tially, precisively, significative, and not insofar as they are
           accidentally, obliquely, significative (cf. 4.43).

T4.600   What then is the meaning of the question, "What is *liter-
           ate?*", undestood in Aristotle's sense?

S4.601   This question can be understood as either *de voce* or *de re*,
           i.e. as being asked about either a word or a circumstance.

S4.602   If the question is understood with reference to the word,
           then *literate* is a word signifying [a] quality (cf. 4.31).

S4.603   If the question is to be understood as having to do with
           circumstances, then [a] *literate* is [a] quality (i.e. literacy).

T4.604   Further, Aristotle's practice was to show circumstances by
           means of words significative, and not merely appellative
           of those circumstances.

S4.610   "*Literate* is [a] quality (i.e. literacy)" can therefore, ac-
           cording to Aristotle's usage, be the answer to a question
           posed either *de voce* or *de re*.

S4.611   Nevertheless it remains true that *literate* is appellative of
           substance.

T4.620   Thus is solved the difficulty (4.21, 4.5022) about the dis-
           crepancy between logicians' spoken usage, and their written
           assertions about, or in connection with, signification: the
           first involves the use of words to refer (appellation), while
           the second is concerned with decisions as to precisive
           signification.

T4.621 The results of neglecting this distinction are just as absurd as those which would result from inferring that a stone must be a male object because *lapis* is a masculine noun, or that to fear is an action because *timere* is an active verb, and so on.

S4.700 A further query: can a single circumstance be assigned to diverse categories? For example, can *literate* be said to signify *having* has well as quality?

T4.710 Tentatively, this may be admitted in those cases where a word signifies things of various categories and those things do not form a single whole: *white* can be said to signify [a] quality and [a] having, but it is appellative of neither; it is in fact appellative of the thing having whiteness.

T4.711 On the other hand *man* signifies and is appellative of a unity, and hence cannot be assigned to diverse categories.

T4.712 But *white* can be said to signify [a] quality and [a] having, because the word is not appellative of quality and having.

S4.713 But (in view of 4.515) in terms of signification alone, can it not be said that *man* signifies [a] substance and [a] quality (cf. 4.22)?

T4.714 *Man* signifies predominantly the qualified substantial unity, whereas *white* has no such dominant unifying feature in its meaning.

T4.72   Elucidation of the meaning of "forms a single whole" (cf. 4.710).

S4.800 Final objections:

S4.801 Could it not be said that *white* signifies *something having whiteness* (and not just . . . *having whiteness* (4.4233)) but indeterminately?

S4.8020 For everything white is something white;

S4.8021 Also *white* signifies something having whiteness or nothing; but nothing cannot have whiteness, therefore *white* must signify *something having whiteness* (4.801).

T4.810   Whether 4.8020 is true or not is not in question here,
            where the discourse moves at a level appropriate to that
            which emerges in a decision as to the signification of forms
            of words.

T4.811   Thus while it may be true that a white is always something
            having whiteness, this fact need not affect the account of
            the signification of *white*.

T4.8120   Indeed, an infinite regress results if *something having
            whiteness* is assumed to be substitutable for *white*.

T4.8121   A similar regress occurs if *that which has whiteness* is
            substituted for *white*.

T4.813   And the argument of 4.8021 is a sophism resting upon a
            misinterpretation of the negation involved in the word
            nothing.

S4.82   Recapitulation of findings in terms of 4.71, with general-
            isation.

T4.83   Reminder of the provisional nature of the conclusions of
            the dialogue.

III

DE GRAMMATICO: TEXT

1.000   DISCIPULUS. De *grammatico* peto ut me certum facias
utrum sit substantia an qualitas, ut hoc cognito, quid de aliis
quae similiter denominative dicuntur sentire debeam, agnoscam.
    MAGISTER. Dic primum cur dubites.
    D. Ideo quia videtur utrumque posse probari necessariis
rationibus, esse scilicet et non esse.
    M. Proba ergo.
    D. Ne ergo festines contradicere quidquid dixero, sed
patere me orationem meam ad suum finem perducere, deinde
aut approba aut corrige.
    M. Ut vis.
1.100   D. Ut quidem
1.101   *grammaticus* probetur esse substantia
sufficit quia
1.11   omnis grammaticus homo, et
1.12   omnis homo substantia.
1.13   Quidquid enim habet grammaticus ut sequatur eum substantia, non habet nisi ex eo quia homo est. Quare hoc concesso ut
homo sit: quaecumque sequuntur *hominem* sequuntur *grammaticum.*

1.20   Quod vero

1.201   *grammaticus* sit qualitas

aperte fatentur philosophi qui de hac re tractaverunt. Quorum auctoritatem de his rebus est impudentia improbare.

1.21   Item quoniam necesse est ut grammaticus sit aut substantia aut qualitas, ut quodlibet horum sit, alterum non sit, et quodlibet non sit, alterum necesse sit esse: quidquid valet ad astruendam unam partem, destruit alteram, et quidquid unam debilitat, alteram roborat. Cum ergo alterum horum verum sit, alterum falsum, rogo ut falsitatem detegens aperias mihi veritatem.

2.00   M.   Argumenta quae ex utraque parte posuisti necessaria sunt, nisi quod dicis: si alterum est, alterum esse non posse. Quare non debes a me exigere, ut alteram partem falsam ostendam — quod ab ullo fieri non potest — sed quomodo sibi invicem non repugnent aperiam, si a me fieri potest. Sed vellem ego prius a te ipso audire, quid his probationibus tuis obici posse opineris.

       D.   Hoc quod tu a me exigis, ego a te intentus expectabam: sed quoniam tu easdem probationes asseris irreprobabiles: meum est qui dubito aperire quid me sollicitet, tuum vero est utriusque partis firmitatem et convenientiam ostendere.

       M.   Dic ergo tu quod sentis, et ego tentabo facere quod poscis.

3.00   D.   Illam quidem propositionem quae dicit grammaticum esse hominem, hoc modo repelli existimo, quia

3.101   nullus grammaticus potest intelligi sine grammatica, et

3.102   omnis homo potest intelligi sine grammatica

3.110   Item:

3.111   omnis grammaticus suscipit magis et minus, et

3.112   nullus homo suscipit magis et minus,

ex qua utraque contextione binarum propositionum conficitur una conclusio, id est:

3.113   nullus grammaticus homo.

3.20   M.   Non consequitur.

          D.   Quare?

3.21   M.   An tibi videtur *animalis* nomen aliquid aliud significare quam *substantiam animatam sensibilem?*

          D.   Prorsus nihil aliud est *animal* quam *substantia animata sensibilis,* nec *substantia animata sensibilis* aliud est quam *animal.*

          M.   Ita est. Sed dic quoque, utrum omne quod non est aliud quam substantia animata sensibilis, possit intelligi praeter rationalitatem, nec sit rationale ex necessitate.

          D.   Negare non possum.

          M.   Omne igitur animal potest intelligi praeter rationalitatem, et nullam animal est ex necessitate rationale.

          D.   Nequeo dicere quin ex concessis consequatur, quamquam valde metuam quod te suspicor intendere.

          M.   At nullus homo potest intelligi praeter rationalitatem, et omnem hominem necesse est rationalem esse.

          D.   Angustiae mihi sunt utrimque. Nam si concedo, concludis nullum hominem esse animal: si renuo, dices me non tantum posse intelligi, sed vere esse sine rationalitate.

          M.   Ne timeas. Non enim sequitur quod putas.

          D.   Si sic est ut promittis, spontaneus concedo quidquid proposuisti; sin autem, invitus.

          M.   Contexe ergo tu ipse quattuor ultimas propositiones quas feci in duos syllogismos.

          D.   Hoc utique ordine digeri possunt:

3.221   Omne animal potest intelligi praeter rationalitatem

3.222   Nullus vero homo potest intelligi praeter rationalitatem.

          Item:

3.231   Nullum animal rationale est ex necessitate

3.232   Omnis autem homo rationalis est ex necessitate.

          Ex utroque hoc ordine binarum propositionum videtur nasci:

3.233   Nullus igitur homo animal est,

          quo nihil falsius, licet praecedentes propositiones in nullo titubare videam.

3.234   Duae namque quae subiectum terminum habent *hominem* [3.222, 3.232] sic sunt per se notae, ut imprudentia sit eas probare; duae vero quae subiciunt *animal* [3.221, 3.231] sic videntur probatae, ut impudentia sit eas negare. Sed video horum duorum syllogismorum conexionem per omnia similem illis duobus quos paulo ante protuli [3.10, 3.11]. Quapropter ad nihil aliud suspicor te hos attulisse, nisi ut cum horum conclusionem aperte falsam cernerem, idem de similibus quos ego feceram decernerem.

M.   Sic est.

D.   Ostende ergo in quo et hic et ibi tanta sit deceptio, ut cum et verae propositiones et secundum naturam syllogismorum conexae videantur, nulla tamen eorum conclusiones veritas tueatur.

3.30   M.   In tuis syllogismis hoc faciam; meos si vis per te discutito.

D.   Fiat tuo iudicio.

3.310   M.   Repete et contexe syllogismos quos fecisti.

3.311   D.   Omnis homo potest intelligi sine grammatica [3.102].

M.   Quid dicis hominem posse intelligi sine grammatica?

D.   Hominem.

M.   Dic ergo in ipsa propositione quod intelligis.

D.   Omnis homo potest intelligi homo sine grammatica.

M.   Concedo; assume.

3.312   D.   Nullus grammaticus potest intelligi sine grammatica [3.101].

M.   Quid non potest grammaticus intelligi sine grammatica?

D.   Grammaticus.

M.   Profer ergo quod intelligis.

D.   Nullus grammaticus potest intelligi grammaticus sine grammatica

3.3121   M.   Iunge has duas propositiones ita integras, sicut eas modo protulisti.

D.   Omnis homo potest intelligi homo sine grammatica [3.311]

Nullus grammaticus potest intelligi grammaticus sine grammatica [3.312].

M. Vide ergo utrum habeant communem terminum, sine quo nihil efficiunt.

D. Video eas non habere communem terminum, et idcirco nihil ex eis consequi.

M. Contexe alterum syllogismum [3.11].

3.320 D. Non iam opus est ut pro eius ostensione labores. Nam adverto eius fallaciam. Sic enim eius propositiones intelligebam, ac si diceretur quia

3.321   nullus homo est magis et minus homo [3.112], et

3.322   omnis grammaticus est magis vel minus grammaticus [3.111].

3.3221 Et quoniam hae duae propositiones nullum habent communem terminum, nihil conficiunt.

M. Itane tibi videtur his tuis conexionibus nihil concludi posse?

D. Ita utique putabam, sed haec tua interrogatio facit me suspectum, ne forte in illis aliqua lateat efficacia. Sed quomodo efficiunt sine communi termino?

3.33 M. Communis terminus syllogismi non tam in prolatione quam in sententia est habendus. Sicut enim nihil efficitur, si communis est in voce et non in sensu: ita nihil obest, si est in intellectu et non in prolatione. Sententia quippe ligat syllogismum, non verba.

3.40 D. Exspecto ut reddas effectum propositionibus meis.

M. Efficiunt vere aliquid, sed non quod expectas.

D. Quidquid illud sit, non ingratus accipio.

M. Qui dicit:
     omnis homo potest intelligi homo sine grammatica [3.102, 3.310] et nullus grammaticus potest intelligi grammaticus sine grammatica [3.101, 3.311],

nonne hoc significat quia

3.41   esse hominis non indiget grammatica, et

3.42   esse grammatici indiget grammatica?

D. Nihil verius.

3.430   M. An habent communem terminum hae duae propositiones [3.41, 3.42] quas modo dixi significari in illis aliis duabus
[3.310, 3.311]?

   D. Habent.

   M. Conficitur ergo quia

3.431   esse grammatici non est esse hominis,

 id est

3.44   non esse eandem definitionem utriusque.

   D. Procul dubio sic video consequi et esse.

3.450   M. Non tamen ideo consequitur

3.451   grammaticum non esse hominem

 sicut tu intelligebas. Sed si ita intelligas

      grammaticus non est homo [3.103,3.113]

 ac si dicatur

3.452   grammaticus non est idem quod homo,

 id est non habent eandem definitionem, vera est conclusio.

3.500   D. Intelligo quod dicis.

   M. Si ergo bene intelligis quae dixi: dic quomodo tu
dissolveres hunc syllogismum, si quis ita contexeret:

3.501   Omnis grammaticus dicitur in eo quod quale.

3.502   Nullus homo dicitur in eo quod quale.

3.503   Nullus igitur homo grammaticus.

3.510   D. Tale mihi hoc videtur esse, ac si diceretur:

3.511   Omne rationale dicitur in eo quod quale,

3.512   At, nullus homo dicitur in eo quod quale.

3.513   Nullus igitur homo rationalis.

Hoc autem nulla probatio verum efficere valet, ut *rationale*
praedicetur de nullo homine.

3.520   Similiter ille syllogismus quem modo protulisti, non necessario concludit *grammaticum* non praedicari de homine. Hoc
enim significant eius propositiones, si secundum veritatem eas
intelligimus, tamquam si diceretur ita:

3.521   Omnis grammaticus dicitur grammaticus in eo quod
      quale [3.501].

3.5220   Nullus homo dicitur homo in eo quod quale [3.502].

3.5221   Ex his autem duabus propositionibus nequaquam consequitur

Nullus grammaticus praedicatur de homine,

quoniam non est idem terminus, qui affirmatur de grammatico et negatur de homine.

3.530   Esset vero in illis communis terminus et necessariam conclusionem ingererent, si aut

3.531   manente propositione sicut posita est [3.521]

sic vera fieret assumptio:

3.532   nullus homo dicitur grammaticus in eo quod quale;

3.5330   aut

3.5331   manente assumptione [3.5220]

sic vere proponeretur:

3.5332   omnis grammaticus dicitur homo in eo quod quale.

Nam ex utraque hac complexione nasceretur quia

3.5333   de nullo homine *grammaticu*s praedicaretur.

3.540   Si quis vero id quod dicitur: homo non est grammaticus, ita velit intelligere, ac si diceretur: homo non est idem quod grammaticus, ut si dicam: fulgor est splendor, aut: fulgor non est splendor, id est, fulgor est idipsum aut non est idipsum quod splendor; si quis, inquam, sic intelligat hoc quod dicitur: homo non est grammaticus: secundum hoc sensum consequitur ex illis propositionibus, si earum vis bene consideretur, quia

3.541   nullus homo est grammaticus.

3.542   Nam ad hoc probandum quia

3.543   essentia hominis non est essentia grammatici

habet earum significatio communem terminum.

3.60   M. Bene intellexisti quid dixi, sed forte non bene considerasti quod dixi.

D. Quomodo bene intellexi, et non bene consideravi?

3.610   M. Dic mihi: si quis sic proponeret:

3.611   nullus homo potest intelligi sine rationalitate,

3.612   omnis autem lapis potest intelligi sine rationalitate;

quid consequeretur?

D. Quid nisi:

3.6121   nullus igitur lapis est homo?

3.620   M.   Quomodo hoc intelligis? An quia

3.621   nullo modo lapis homo,

an quia

3.622   non est lapis idem quod homo?

D.   Quia nullo modo lapis est homo.

3.630   M.   Dic ergo: quid differt iste syllogismus [3.61] ab illo
tuo syllogismo [3.10], in quo dicis grammaticum non posse intelligi sine grammatica, hominem vero posse, et ideo grammaticum
hominem non esse?

3.631   D.   Quantum quidem ad vim argumentationis, nihil video
hunc ab illo differre. Sicut enim ibi intelligendum est quia grammaticus non potest intelligi grammaticus sine grammatica, et
homo potest intelligi homo sine grammatica; ita hic est intelligendum quia

3.6311   homo non potest intelligi homo sine rationalitate,

et

3.6312   lapis potest intelligi lapis sine rationalitate;

3.6313   et idcirco cum huius syllogismi sit rata conclusio, quia
nullo modo lapis est homo [cf. 3.62]: videris mihi syllogismi mei,
qui omnino similis est isti, conclusionem callidis tuis expositioni-
bus obruisse. Unde iam intelligo quid dixeris quia bene intellexi,
sed non bene consideravi. Bene enim intellexi quid loquendo
mihi significares, sed idipsum quod significabas non bene consideravi, quia quomodo me deciperet ignoravi.

3.6320   M.   Immo in hoc non bene considerasti, quia quomodo
te non deciperet ignorasti.

D.   Quomodo?

M.   Quippe si iste syllogismus quem modo [3.61] proposui
sic exponatur quemadmodum exposui tuum [3.10], ut dicatur:

nullus homo potest intelligi homo sine rationalitate
[3.6311]

omnis autem lapis potest intelligi lapis sine rationalitate [3.6312],

non habebit aliam vim concludendi, quam dixi tuum habere. Sed
quoniam iste quodam alio modo potest intelligi quo ille tuus non

potest, habet hanc conclusionem, ut nullo modo lapis homo esse possit. Cum enim dico quia

> nullus homo intelligi valet sine rationalitate [3.611]

et

> omnis lapis valet intelligi sine rationalitate [3.612],

sic potest immo debet accipi ac si dicatur:

3.6321   nullus homo potest aliquo modo intelligi sine rationalitate

3.6322   omnis vero lapis quolibet modo potest intelligi sine rationalitate.

Unde conficitur:

3.63221   nullus igitur lapis aliquo modo est homo.

3.6330   In tuis vero propositionibus [3.10] veritas nequaquam similem admittit subauditionem. Namque non potest dici quia

3.6331   nullus grammaticus intelligi valet aliquo modo sine grammatica, aut

3.6332   omnis homo valet quolibet modo intelligi sine grammatica.

Nam et

3.6333   omnis qui grammaticus est, potest intelligi homo sine grammatica, et

3.6334   nullus homo potest intelligi grammaticus sine grammatica.

3.6340   Quapropter non possunt conficere

3.6341   grammaticum nequaquam esse hominem.

3.700   D. Non habeo quid contra hanc tuam sententiam dicam. Sed quoniam latenter monuisti me ut non sim contentus intelligere quid dicas, sed idipsum quod dicis considerem: videtur mihi consideranda illa conclusio quam ex meo syllogismo confici ostendisti, quia

> esse grammatici non est esse hominis [3.431].

3.701   Si enim hoc [3.431] est, qui habet essentiam grammatici non ideo necessario habet essentiam hominis. Sed

3.71   si *homo* sequitur *grammaticum*, essentia hominis sequitur essentiam grammatici. Sed

3.711   haec non sequitur hanc. Quare nec ille illum.

3.7111   Non est igitur omnis grammaticus homo.

3.72   At cum omnibus grammaticis una sit ratio cur sint homines; profecto

             aut omnis grammaticus est homo, aut nullus.

3.721   Sed constat quia

             non omnis.

3.7211   Nullus igitur.

Videtur itaque quia syllogismo meo conclusionem quam acute abstulisti, auferendo acutius dedisti.

3.800   M. Etsi latenter te monui considerare quod audis, non tamen ut apparet inutiliter. Nam etsi sophistice probes nullum grammaticum hominem per hoc quod esse grammatici non est esse hominis; utile tamen tibi erit, cum ipsum sophisma quod te sub pallio verae rationis fallit, in sua fallacia nudum conspicies.

      D. Ostende ergo quod me fallat et ubi me fallat haec [3.7] quam modo feci de grammatico probatio.

      M. Redeamus iterum ad *animal* et *hominem,* in quibus ita quasi palpamus veritatem, ut nullum sophisma nobis persuadeat licet cogat credere falsitatem. Dic ergo utrum esse uniuscuisque rei in definitione consistat.

      D. Ita est.

      M. Definitio hominis est definitio animalis?

3.8010   D. Minime. Si enim *animal rationale mortale* quae est definitio hominis, esset definitio animalis: cuicumque conveniret *animal* conveniret *rationale mortale,*

3.8011   quod falsum est.

3.8012   M. Non est igitur esse hominis esse animalis.

      D. Ita consequitur.

3.810   M. Potes igitur ex hoc probare quia

3.811   nullus homo animal est,

eadem ratione qua probasti modo [3.7] nullum grammaticum hominem. Quapropter si vides apertam esse falsitatem, quod haec tua ratiocinatio hic concludit: ne credas certam esse veritatem quod ibi ludit.

3.900   D. Iam ostendisti quia me fallit; ostende etiam ubi.

M.   Non tenes quod paulo ante [3.4] dixi te concedente quia

esse grammatici non est esse hominis [3.431] idem valet ac si diceretur

definitio grammatici non est definitio hominis [3.44], id est

3.901   non est idem omnino grammaticus et homo?
sicut enim *homo* definiri non debet cum grammatica, ita *grammaticus* non valet sine grammatica [cf. 3.41, 3.42].

3.910   Quare debet intelligi illa tua argumentatio hoc modo:

3.911   Si esse grammatici non est simpliciter esse hominis, qui habet essentiam grammatici, non ideo consequitur ut habeat simpliciter essentiam hominis [cf. 3.701].

3.920   Similiter intelligendum est quia

3.921   simpliciter *homo* non sequitur *grammaticum* [3.71, 3.711]

id est:

3.922   si grammaticus est, non consequitur ut sit simpliciter homo.

3.930   Ita vero nihil aliud consequitur nisi:

3.931   nullus grammaticus est simpliciter homo.

D.   Nihil clarius.

3.940   M.   Verum si probaretur, quod ut puto facile fieri potest, quia

3.9410   esse grammatici ita non est esse hominis
3.9411   sicut esse albi non est esse hominis
3.9412   — potest enim homo esse sine albo et album sine homine —

3.9420   tunc vere consequeretur

3.9421   aliquem grammaticum posse esse non hominem.

D.   Quid ergo laboramus, si hoc probari potest? Proba, et finiatur haec quaestio.

3.9430   M.   Non hoc a me debes exigere. Non enim in hac quaestione ventilamus utrum possit esse, sed utrum

3.9431   sit aliquis grammaticus non homo,
quod vides monstrari non posse.

4.100   D.   Nondum video, quia adhuc habeo dicere contra.
        M.   Dic.
        D.   Aristoteles ostendit
4.101   grammaticum eorum esse quae sunt in subiecto.
4.102   Et nullus homo est in subiecto.
4.103   Quare nullus grammaticus homo [cf. 1.11].
4.1100 M.   Noluit Aristoteles hoc consequi ex suis dictis. Nam idem
        Aristoteles dicit et quendam hominem, et hominem et animal
        grammaticum.
        D.   Quomodo ergo dissolvitur iste syllogismus?
4.1101 M.   Responde mihi: cum loqueris mihi de grammatico,
        unde intelligam te loqui: de hoc nomine, an de rebus quas signifi-
        cat?
        D.   De rebus.
        M.   Quas ergo res significat?
        D.   Hominem et grammaticam.
4.1102 M.   Audito ergo hoc nomine, intelligam *hominem* aut
        grammaticam, et
4.1103 loquens de grammatico, loquar de homine aut de gram-
        matica.
        D.   Ita oportet.
4.1104 M.   Dic ergo: homo est substantia, an in subiecto?
        D.   Non est in subiecto, sed est substantia.
4.1105 M.   Grammatica est qualitas, et in subiecto?
        D.   Utrumque est.
        M.   Quid ergo mirum si quis dicit quia
4.111   grammaticus est substantia et non est in subiecto secundum
        hominem, et
4.112   grammaticus est qualitas et in subiecto secundum gram-
        maticam?

4.1200 D.   Diffiteri non possum. Sed unum adhuc dicam cur
        grammaticus non sit substantia:
4.1201 quia omnis substantia est prima aut secunda, grammaticus
        autem nec prima nec secunda.

M. Memento dictorum Aristotelis quae paulo ante [4.11-00] dixi, quibus dicit grammaticum et primam et secundam substantiam, quia et quendam hominem, et hominem et animal grammaticum dici testatur. Sed tamen unde probas grammaticum non esse primam nec secundam substantiam?

4.121 D. Quia est in subiecto, quod nulla substantia est; et dicitur de pluribus, quod primae non est;

4.122 nec est genus aut species nec dicitur in eo quod quid, quod est secundae.

4.130 M. Nihil horum si bene meministi quae iam diximus aufert grammatico substantiam, quia

4.131 secundum aliquid grammaticus non est in subiecto, et est genus et species, et dicitur in eo quod quid; quia est et homo qui species est, et animal quod est genus, et haec dicuntur in eo quod quid [cf. 4.122].

4.132 Est etiam individuus, sicut homo et animal, quia quemadmodum quidam homo et quoddam animal, ita quidam grammaticus est individuus. Socrates enim et animal et homo est, et grammaticus [cf. 4.121].

D. Non possum negare quod dicis.

4.14 M. Si alia non habes unde possis probare grammaticum non esse hominem: nunc proba eum non esse grammaticam.

D. Facilius hoc possum digito quam argumento. Ibi namque fregisti omnia mea argumenta, ubi aperuisti a *grammatico* significari diversa, et secundum ea loquendum intelligendumque de grammatico. Quod quamvis abnuere non possim, tamen non sic satisfacit animo meo ut velut quod quaerebat invento quiescat. Videris enim mihi quasi non curare ut me doceas, sed tantum ut rationes meas obstruas. Sed sicut meum fuit exponere quae me ex utraque parte in ambiguitatem cogunt: ita tuum erat aut unam partem destruere, aut ostendere quomodo non sibi invicem repugnent.

M. Cur non satis tibi videtur ostensum, quod *grammaticum* esse substantiam et grammaticum esse qualitatem nequaquam sibi repugnent invicem, in eo quod de grammatico modo secundum hominem, modo secundum grammaticam loqui et intelligere oportet?

4.20   D.   Quoniam nemo qui intelligit nomen grammatici ignorat
grammaticum significare hominem et grammaticam, et tamen si
hac fiducia loquens in populo dicam: utilis scientia est grammaticus, aut: bene scit homo iste grammaticum: non solum
stomachabuntur grammatici, sed et ridebunt rustici.

4.210   Nullatenus itaque credam sine aliqua alia ratione tractatores
dialecticae tam saepe et tam studiose in suis libris scripsisse, quod
idem ipsi colloquentes dicere erubescerent.

4.211   Saepissime namque cum volunt ostendere qualitatem aut
accidens, subiungunt: ut *grammaticus* et similia,

4.212   cum *grammaticum* magis esse substantiam quam qualitatem
aut accidens usus omnium loquentium attestetur. Et cum volunt
aliquid docere de substantia, nusquam proferunt: ut *grammaticus*
aut aliquid huiusmodi.

4.22   Huc accedit, quia si ideo *grammaticus* quia significat
hominem et grammaticam dicendus est substantia et qualitas: cur
homo non est similiter qualitas et substantia? *Homo* namque
significat substantiam cum omnibus illis differentiis quae sunt in
homine, ut est sensibilitas et mortalitas. Sed nusquam ubi scriptum
sit aliquid de qualitate aliqua, prolatum est ad exemplum: velut
homo.

4.230   M.   Quod illam rationem quam dixi, cur grammaticus scilicet sit substantia et qualitas, idcirco repudias quia non valet in
nomine hominis: ideo facis, ut puto, quia non consideras quam
dissimiliter significent scilicet nomen hominis ea ex quibus constat
homo, et *grammaticus* hominem et grammaticam.

4.231   Nempe nomen hominis per se et ut unum significat ea ex
quibus constat totus homo. In quibus substantia principalem locum
tenet, quoniam est causa aliorum et habens ea, non ut indigens
illis, sed ut se indigentia. Nulla enim est differentia substantiae
sine qua substantia inveniri non possit, et nulla differentiarum
eius sine illa potest existere. Quapropter quamvis omnia simul
velut unum totum sub una significatione uno nomine appellentur
homo, sic tamen principaliter hoc nomen est significativum et appellativum substantiae, ut cum recte dicatur: substantia est homo
et homo substantia: nullus tamen dicat: rationalitas est homo
aut homo rationalitas, sed habens rationalitatem.

4.232 *Grammaticus* vero non significat hominem et grammaticum ut unum, sed grammaticam per se et hominem per aliud significat.

4.233 Et hoc nomen quamvis sit appellativum hominis, non tamen proprie dicitur eius significativum;

4.2340 et licet sit significativum grammaticae, non tamen est eius appellativum.

4.2341 Appellativum autem nomen cuiuslibet rei nunc dico, quo res ipsa usu loquendi appellatur. Nullo enim usu loquendi dicitur: grammatica est grammaticus, aut: grammaticus est grammatica; sed homo est grammaticus, et grammaticus homo.

4.240 D. Non video quid dicas quia *grammaticus* significat grammaticam per se, et hominem per aliud, et quomodo grammaticae tantum sit significativum. Sicut enim *homo* constat ex *animali* et *rationalitate et mortalitate,* et idcirco homo significat haec tria: ita *grammaticus* constat ex *homine* et *grammatica,* et ideo nomen hoc significat utrumque. Numquam enim dicitur grammaticus aut homo sine grammatica, aut grammatica sine homine.

M. Si ergo ita est ut tu dicis, definitio et esse grammatici est: homo sciens grammaticam.

D. Non potest aliud esse.

4.2411 M. Ergo cum grammatica dividit hominem grammaticum a non-grammatico, conducit grammaticum ad esse, et est pars eius quod est esse rei, nec potest adesse et abesse a grammatico praeter subiecti corruptionem.

D. Quid inde?

M. Non est igitur grammatica accidens sed substantialis differentia, et est homo genus, et grammaticus species. Nec dissimilis est ratio de albedine et similibus accidentibus. Quod falsum esse totius artis tractatus ostendit.

D. Quamquam non possim negare quod dicis, nondum tamen mihi persuasum est quod *grammaticus* non significet hominem.

4.2412 M. Ponamus quod sit aliquod animal rationale — non tamen homo — quod ita sciat grammaticam sicut homo.

D. Facile est hoc fingere.

M. Est igitur aliquis non-homo sciens grammaticam.

D. Ita sequitur.

M.   At omme sciens grammaticam est grammaticum.

D.   Concedo.

M.   Est igitur quidam non-homo grammaticus.

D.   Consequitur.

M.   Sed tu dicis in grammatico intelligi hominem.

D.   Dico.

M.   Quidam igitur non-homo est homo, quod falsum est.

D.   Ad hoc ratio deducitur.

4.24121 M.   Nonne ergo vides quia *grammaticus* non ob aliud magis videtur significare *hominem* quam *albus*, nisi quia grammatica soli homini accidit, albedo vero non soli homini?

D.   Sic sequitur ex eo quod finximus. Sed sine figmento volo ut hoc efficias.

4.2413 M.   Si *homo* est in *grammatico*, non praedicatur cum eo simul de aliquo, sicut *animal* non praedicatur cum homine, quia inest in *homine*. Non enim apte dicitur quia Socrates est homo animal.

D.   Non potest contradici.

M.   Sed convenienter dicitur quia Socrates est homo grammaticus.

D.   Convenienter.

M.   Non est igitur *homo* in *grammatico*.

D.   Sic consequi video.

4.2414 M.   Item si *grammaticus* est *homo sciens grammaticam*, ubicumque ponitur *grammaticus*, apte ponitur *homo sciens grammaticam*.

D.   Ita est.

M.   Si igitur apte dicitur: Socrates est homo grammaticus, apte quoque dicitur: Socrates est homo homo sciens grammaticam.

D.   Consequitur.

M.   Omnis autem homo sciens grammaticam est homo grammaticus.

D.   Ita est.

M.   Socrates igitur qui est homo homo sciens grammaticam, est homo homo grammaticus. Et quoniam grammaticus est homo sciens grammaticam, consequitur ut Socrates sit homo homo homo sciens grammaticam, et sic in infinitum.

    D.   Non possum apertae consequentiae resistere.

4.2415   M.   Item si in *grammatico, homo* intelligendus est cum *grammatica,* intelligendum est similiter in omnibus similibus denominativis id quod denominatur cum eo a quo denominatur.

    D.   Hoc sentiebam.

    M.   Ergo *hodiernum* significat id quod vocatur *hodiernum* et *hodie.*

    D.   Quid postea?

    M.   *Hodiernum* igitur significat aliquid cum tempore.

    D.   Ita esse necesse est.

    M.   Igitur *hodiernum* non est nomen sed verbum, quia est vox consignificans tempus, nec est oratio.

4.30   D.   Satis mihi probasti *grammaticum* non significare *hominem.*

    M.   Vides igitur quid dixerim quia *grammaticus* non est *hominis* significativum? [4.233]

    D.   Video, et exspecto ut *grammaticum* ostendas esse significativum *grammaticae.*

4.31   M.   Nonne paulo ante dicebas *grammaticum* significare *hominem scientem grammaticam?* [4.240]

    D.   Et credebam.

    M.   Sed iam satis probatum est quia non significat *hominem.*

    D.   Satis.

    M.   Quid ergo restat?

    D.   Ut non significet aliud quam *scientem grammaticam.*

    M.   Est igitur significativum *grammaticae.*

4.40   D.   Sufficienter probatum est

4.411   *grammaticum* non esse appellativum grammaticae sed hominis [cf.4.233.234]

4.412   nec esse significativum *hominis* sed *grammaticae* [cf.4.232.-233].

4.413   Sed quoniam dixisti *grammaticum* significare *grammaticam* per se et *hominem* per aliud [cf. 4.232] peto ut aperte mihi duas has significationes distinguas ut intelligam

4.414   quomodo *grammaticus* non sit significativum eius quod aliquo modo significat, aut

4.415   quomodo sit apellativum eius cuius significativum non est.

4.4210   M.   Si est in domo aliqua albus equus te nesciente inclusus, et aliquis tibi dicit: in hac domo est album sive albus; an scis per hoc ibi esse equum?

D.   Non. Sive enim dicat album albedinem, sive in quo est albedo: nullius certae rei mente concipio essentiam nisi huius coloris.

M.   Etiamsi aliquid aliud intelligis quam colorem istum: illud tamen certum est, quia eius in quo est ipse color essentiam per hoc nomen non intelligis.

4.4211   D.   Certum. Nam etsi occurrat animo corpus aut superficies, quod non ob aliud fit nisi quia expertus sum in his solere esse albedinem: ipsum tamen nomen albi nihil horum significat, sicut probatum est de *grammatico*. Sed adhuc exspecto ut ostendas quia significat.

4.422   M.   Quid si vides stantes iuxta se invicem album equum et nigrum bovem, et dicit tibi aliquis de equo: *percute illum,* non monstrans aliquo signo de quo dicat: an scis quod de equo dicat?

D.   Non.

M.   Si vero nescienti tibi et interroganti: *quem?* respondet: *album,* intelligis de quo dicit?

D.   Equum intelligo per nomen albi.

M.   Nomen igitur albi significat tibi equum.

D.   Significat utique.

M.   Nonne vides quia alio modo quam nomen equi?

4.4231   D.   Video. Nempe nomen equi etiam priusquam sciam ipsum equum album esse, significat mihi equi substantiam per se, et non per aliud.

4.4232   Nomen vero albi substantiam significat non per se, sed per aliud, id est per hoc quia scio equum esse album.

4.4233   Cum enim nihil aliud significet hoc nomen, quod est *albus,* quam haec oratio, quae est *habens albedinem:* sicut haec oratio per se constituit mihi intellectum albedinis, et non eius rei quae habet albedinem; ita et nomen.

4.4234 Sed quoniam scio albedinem esse in equo, et hoc per aliud quam per nomen albi, velut per visum: intellecta albedine per hoc nomen, intelligo equum per hoc quod albedinem scio esse in equo, id est per aliud quam per nomen albi, quo tamen equus appellatur.

4.424 M. Vides ergo quomodo *albus* non sit significativum eius quod aliquo modo significat, et quomodo sit appellativum eius cuius non est significativum?

D. Hoc quoque video. Significat enim equum et non significat,

4.4241 quia non eum significat per se, sed per aliud, et tamen equus appellatur albus.

4.4242 Et quod video in *albo,* hoc intelligo in *grammatico,* et in similibus denominativis.

4.4243 Quapropter videtur mihi significatio nominum et verborum sic dividi posse, quod alia sit per se, alia per aliud.

4.430 M. Considera etiam, quoniam harum duarum significationum illa quae per se est, ipsis vocibus significativis est substantialis, altera vero accidentalis.

4.431 Cum enim in definitione nominis vel verbi dicitur quia est vox significativa, intelligendum est non alia significatione quam ea quae per se est. Nam si illa significatio quae est per aliud, in definitione nominis vel verbi intelligenda est, iam non erit *hodiernus* nomen sed verbum [cf. 4.2415]. Significat enim aliquando ea significatione aliquid cum tempore, sicut supra dixi, quod non est nominis sed verbi.

4.500 D. Patet quod dicis.

4.501 Sed non sine scrupulo accipit animus *grammaticum* esse qualitatem, quamvis significet grammaticam,

4.5020 aut hominem solum, id est sine grammatica, esse grammaticum,

4.5021 licet probatum sit hominem simul et grammaticam non esse grammaticum; unde consequitur solum hominem esse grammaticum, quoniam non potest esse grammaticus nisi aut solus aut cum grammatica.

4.5022   Quamvis namque grammatici nomen significativum sit grammaticae: non tamen convenienter respondetur quaerenti quid grammaticus sit: *grammatica,* aut *qualitas.*

4.503   Et si nullus est grammaticus nisi participando grammaticam, consequitur ut homo non sit grammaticus nisi cum grammatica.

4.510   M. Quod quidem dicitur quia homo solus, id est sine grammatica, est grammaticus, quantum ad tuam quaestionem solvendum sifficit, duobus modis intelligi potest, uno vero, altero falso.

4.511   Homo quippe solus sine grammatica est grammaticus, quia solus est habens grammaticam. Grammatica namque nec sola nec cum homine habet grammaticam.

4.5120   Sed homo solus, id est absque grammatica, non est grammaticus, quia absente grammatica nullus esse grammaticus potest.

4.5121   Sicut qui praecedendo ducit alium, et solus est praevius, quia qui sequitur non est praevius, nec separatim nec sic ut ex illis duobus unus fiat praevius; et solus non est praevius, quia nisi sit qui sequatur, praevius esse non potest.

4.5122   Cum vero dicitur quia grammaticus est qualitas: non recte nisi secundum tractatum Aristotelis *De Categoriis* dicitur.

4.513   D. An aliud habet ille tractatus quam: omne quod est aut est substantia aut quantitas aut qualitas et cetera? Si igitur solus homo est grammaticus, sola substantia est grammaticus. Quomodo ergo secundum illum tractatum magis est grammaticus qualitas quam substantia?

4.5141   M. Etsi hoc ibi intelligatur quod tu dicis, quia omne quod est aliquid horum est: non tamen fuit principalis intentio Aristotelis hoc in illo libro ostendere, sed quoniam omne nomen vel verbum aliquid horum significat.

4.5142   Non enim intendebat ostendere quid sint singulae res, nec quarum rerum sint appellativae singulae voces: sed quarum significativae sint.

4.5143   Sed quoniam voces non significant nisi res; dicendo quid sit quod voces significant, necesse fuit dicere quid sint res.

4.5144   Nam ut alia taceam, sufficienter hoc quod dico divisio quam facit in principio tractatus *Categoriarum* ostendit. Non enim ait: eorum quae sunt, singulum est aut substantia aut quantitas et cetera; nec ait: eorum quae secundum nullam complexionem dicuntur, singulum aut substantia appellatur aut quantitas, sed ait: eorum quae secundum nullam complexionem dicuntur, singulum aut substantiam significat aut quantitatem.

D.   Persuadet ratio quod dicis.

4.515   M.   Cum ergo Aristoteles ita dicat: eorum quae secundum nullam complexionem dicuntur, singulum aut substantiam significat aut quantitatem, et cetera: de qua significatione videtur tibi dicere, de illa quae per se significant ipsae voces et quae illis est substantialis, an de altera quae per aliud est et accidentalis?

D.   Non nisi de illa quam idem ipse eisdem vocibus inesse definiendo nomen et verbum assignavit, qua per se significant.

M.   An putas illum aliter prosecutum in tractatu, quam proposuit in divisione, aut aliquem eorum qui eum sequentes de dialectica scripserunt, aliter sentire voluisse de hac re, quam ipse sensit?

D.   Nullo modo eorum scripta hoc aliquem opinari permittunt, quia nusquam invenitur aliquis eorum posuisse aliquam vocem ad ostendendum aliquid quod significet per aliud, sed semper ad hoc quod per se significat. Nullus enim volens monstrare substantiam ponit *album* aut *grammaticum*, sed de qualitate docens *album* et *grammaticum* profert, et similia.

4.600   M.   Si ergo proposita divisione praefata quaero a te quid sit *grammaticus* secundum hanc divisionem et secundum eos qui illam scribendo de dialectica sequuntur: quid quaero, aut quid mihi respondebis?

4.601   D.   Procul dubio non hic potest quaeri nisi aut de voce aut de re quam significat. Quare quia constat *grammaticum* non significare secundum hanc divisionem *hominem* sed *grammaticam*, incunctanter respondebo:

4.602   se quaeris de voce, quia est vox significans qualitatem;

4.603   si vero quaeris de re, quia est qualitas.

4.604   M. An ignoras quia idem Aristoteles appellat voces nomine rerum quarum sunt significativae, et non quarum tantum sunt appellativae, in eodem libro; ut cum dicit quia omnis substantia videtur significare hoc aliquid, id est omnis vox significans substantiam? Sicut nominat vel potius ostendit res — quod tu paulo ante meministi — solis vocibus earum significativis et saepe non appellativis.

4.610   D. Non hoc ignorare possum. Quare sive quaeretur de voce sive de re; cum quaeritur quid sit *grammaticus* secundum tractatum Aristotelis et secundum sequaces eius, recte respondetur: qualitas;

4.611   et tamen secundum appellationem vere est substantia.

4.620   M. Ita est. Non enim movere nos debet quod dialectici aliter scribunt de vocibus secundum quod sunt significativae, aliter eis utuntur loquendo secundum quod sunt appellativae, si et grammatici aliud dicunt secundum formam vocum, aliud secundum rerum naturam.

4.621   Dicunt quippe *lapidem* esse masculini generis, *petram* feminini, *mancipium* autem neutri, et *timere* activum, *timeri* vero passivum, cum nemo dicat esse lapidem masculum aut petram feminam, aut mancipium nec masculum nec feminam, aut timere facere, timeri autem pati.

4.700   D. Aperta ratio nihil me in iis quae dixisti dubitare permittit. Sed adhuc est de hac quaestione quod velim discere. Nam si *grammaticus* est qualitas quia significat qualitatem, non video cur *armatus* non sit substantia cum significet substantiam. Et si *armatus* ideo est *habere* quia significat habere, ignoro cur *grammaticus* non sit *habere* quia significat habere. Omnino enim quemadmodum *grammaticus* probatur significare qualitatem, quia significat *habentem qualitatem,* ita *armatus* significat substantiam, quia significat *habentem substantiam,* id est arma. Et sicut *armatus* convincitur significare habere, quia significat *habentem arma,* sic *grammaticus* significat habere, quia significat *habentem disciplinam.*

M. Nullatenus hac ratione considerata negare possum aut *armatum* esse substantiam aut *grammaticum* habere.

D. Vellem ergo a te doceri utrum unum aliquid possit esse diversorum praedicamentorum.

4.710 M. Rem quidem unam eandemque non puto sub diversis aptari posse praedicamentis, licet in quibusdam dubitari possit; quod maiori et altiori indigere disputatione existimo, quam hac nostra brevi sermocinatione assumpsimus. Unam autem vocem plura significantem non ut unum, non video quid prohibeat pluribus aliquando supponi praedicamentis, ut si *albus* dicitur qualitas et habere. *Albus* enim non ita significat qualitatem et habere ut unum, quemadmodum *homo* significat ut unum substantiam et qualitates quibus constat homo. Res enim quae appellatur *homo* est unum quiddam constans ex iis quae dixi; res vero quae appellatur *albus* non est unum aliquid ex habere et qualitate constans, quia nihil appellatur *albus* nisi res quae habet albedinem, quae nequaquam constat ex habere et qualitate.

4.711 Quare si dicitur: homo est substantia et homo est qualitas, una eademque res quae significatur et appellatur hoc nomine, dicitur substantia esse et qualitas, quod videtur inconveniens.

4.712 Cum autem dicimus quia albus est qualitas et habere, non dicimus quia quod appellatur hoc nomine est qualitas et habere, sed quia haec duo significantur hoc nomine et nihil inconveniens sequitur.

4.713 D. Cur autem non est homo secundum divisionem Aristotelis substantia et qualitas, quia utrumque significat, quemadmodum est albus qualitas et habere propter utriusque significationem?

4.714 M. Aestimo huic interrogationi illud posse sufficere quod supra dixi, quia principaliter est significativum substantiae, et quia unum illud quod significat substantia est, et non qualitas sed quale; albus vero nihil principalius sed pariter significat qualitatem et habere, nec fit unum ex his quod magis sit hoc vel illud, cuius sit *albus* significativum.

4.72 D. Planius mihi vellem explicari quomodo non fiat unum aliquid ex iis quae significat *albus*.

M.　Si aliquid constat ex eis, aut est substantia aut aliquid aliorum praedicamentorum.

D.　Aliud esse non potest.

M.　Sed nihil horum fit ex habere et albedine.

D.　Non possum contradicere.

M.　Item: unum non fit ex pluribus nisi aut compositione partium quae sunt eiusdem praedicamenti, ut animal constat corpore et anima; aut convenientia generis et differentiae unius vel plurium, ut corpus et homo; aut specie et proprietatum collectione, ut Plato. Illa vero quae albus significat, non sunt unius praedicamenti, nec est alterum alteri genus aut differentia aut species aut collectio proprietatum, nec sunt differentiae unius generis, sed sunt accidentia eiusdem subiecti, quod tamen subiectum *albus* non significat, quia omnino nihil significat aliud quam habere et qualitatem. Quare non fit unum ex iis quae *albus* significat.

4.800　　D.　Quamquam ratio mihi asserere videatur quae disseris, vellem tamen audire quid responderes, si quis ad hoc quod dicis quia nihil omnino significat *albus* aliud quam habere et qualitatem, sic obiceret:

4.801　　*Albus* cum sit idem quod habens albedinem, non significat determinate hoc vel illud habens, velut corpus, sed indeterminate aliquid habens albedinem.

4.8020　　Albus enim aut est qui habet albedinem, aut qui non habet. Sed qui non habet albedinem, non est albus. Albus igitur est qui habet albedinem. Quare quoniam omnis qui albedinem habet non nisi aliquid est, necesse est ut albus sit aliquid quod habet albedinem, aut aliquid habens albedinem.

4.8021　　Denique *albus* aut aliquid significat habens albedinem aut nihil. Sed nihil non potest intelligi habens albedinem. Necesse est ergo ut *albus* significet aliquid habens albedinem.

4.810　　M.　Non agitur utrum omnis qui est albus sit aliquid aut sit qui habet, sed utrum hoc nomen sua significatione contineat hoc quod dicitur aliquid aut qui habet — sicut *homo* continet *animal* — ut quomodo *homo* est *animal rationale mortale*, ita albus sit *aliquid habens albedinem* aut *qui habet albedinem*.

4.811 Multa namque necesse est rem quamlibet esse, quae tamen rei eiusdem nomine non significantur. Nam omne animal necesse est coloratum esse et rationale aut irrationale, nomen tamen animalis nihil horum significat. Quare licet albus non sit nisi aliquid habens aut qui habet albedinem, non tamen necesse est ut *albus* hoc significet.

4.8120 Ponamus enim quod *albus* sive *album* significet *aliquid habens albedinem.* Sed aliquid habens albedinem non est aliud quam *aliquid album.*

D. Non potest aliud esse.

M. *Albus* igitur sive *album* semper significat *aliquid album.*

D. Ita sit.

M. Ubi ergo ponitur *albus* vel *album*, recte semper accipitur pro *albo, aliquid album.*

D. Consequitur.

M. Ergo ubi dicitur *aliquid album*, recte quoque dicitur bis: *aliquid aliquid album;* et ubi bis, ibi et ter, et hoc infinite.

D. Consequens et absurdum est hoc.

4.8121 M. Sit quoque *albus* idipsum quod est *qui albedinem habet.* Sed *habet* non est aliud quam *habens est.*

D. Nec potest esse.

M. *Albus* ergo non est aliud quam *qui albedinem habens est.*

D. Non aliud.

M. Cum autem dicitur *albedinem habens*, non aliud significat haec oratio quam *album.*

D. Ita est.

M. Idem igitur est *albus* quod *qui albus est.*

D. Sic sequitur.

M. Ubicumque itaque ponitur *albus*, recte pro eo accipitur: *qui albus est.*

D. Non possum negare.

M. Si ergo *albus* est *qui albus est*, est etiam *qui qui albus est est.* Et si hoc est, est etiam *qui qui qui albus est est est*, et sic in infinitum.

D. Nec hoc minus consequens nec minus absurdum est quam ut saepe sit *aliquid aliquid.*

4.813   M. Si quis autem dicit quia *albus* aut aliquid significat
habens albedinem aut nihil: si sic intelligitur, ac si diceretur: *albus*
aut significat aliquid habens aut significat non-aliquid habens,
ut non-aliquid sit infinitum nomen, non est integra nec vera divisio,
et ideo nihil probat. Veluti si quis diceret, *Caecus aut videt aliquid*
aut videt non-aliquid. Si vero sic intelligitur, quia aut significat
aliquid habens aut non significat: integra est divisio et vera, nec
repugnat iis quae dicta sunt.

4.82   D. Satis apparet quia per *album* non significatur *aliquid*
habens albedinem nec *qui albedinem habet,* sed tantum *albedinem*
habens, id est qualitas et habere, ex quibus solis non conficitur
unum aliquid, et ideo *albus* est utrumque, quia pariter utrumque
significat. Quam rationem in omnibus quae sine complexione
dicuntur et similiter significant quamlibet plura ex quibus non
fit unum, valere video; nec aliquid iis quae in hac disputatione
asseruisti, obici recte posse existimo.

4.83   M. Nec mihi nunc videtur. Tamen quoniam scis quantum
nostris temporibus dialectici certent de quaestione a te proposita,
nolo te sic iis quae diximus inhaerere, ut ea pertinaciter teneas, si
quis validioribus argumentis haec destruere et diversa valuerit
astruere. Quod si contingerit: saltem ad exercitationem dis-
putandi nobis haec profecisse non negabis.

DIALOGUE ON PARONYMS: TRANSLATION

1.000   STUDENT. I'd like you to clear up for me the question
as to whether *literate* is substance or quality, so that when I've
appreciated this example, I'll know how I ought to view other
things which, like a literate, are spoken of paronymously.

         TUTOR. First tell me why you're undecided.

         S. Because it looks as though cogent reasons are avail-
able which both prove and disprove either alternative.

         T. State them.

S. On condition that you won't be too quick in disagreeing with everything I have to say; let me finish my piece before you concur or correct.

T. As you will.

1.100   D. To prove that

1.101   *literate* is [a] substance

one only needs the following premisses:

1.11   Every literate is [a] man

1.12   Every man is [a] substance.

1.13   For a literate has that from which his substantiality ensues, whatever it may be, only on account of his being a man; so granted that [a] literate is [a] man, the same things may be inferred from *literate* as from *man*.

1.20   On the other hand the philosophers who have written about this business obviously believe that

1.201   *literate* is [a] quality

and one can hardly disregard their authority in these matters.

1.21   Again, *literate* must be substance or quality, in such a way that if one of these alternatives holds, the other does not hold, and if one of them does not hold, the other must hold; correspondingly, whatsoever serves to establish the one alternative, refutes the other, and whatsoever weakens the one strengthens the other. Now as only one of the two can hold, I'd like you to pin-point the falsehood and so clear up the case for me.

2.00   T. The points you urge in favor of both alternatives are cogent, but not your assertion that if the one holds the other cannot. So you shouldn't ask me to show the falsity of one or the other of the two — this just can't be done — but rather, if I can manage it, I'll make clear how they can be compatible. However, first of all I'd like to hear what you think might constitute objections to the arguments you brought forward.

S. You're asking me to take on exactly the task which I was keen that you should perform; but as you assert that the arguments in question are in order, it's up to me, as the doubter, to disclose the qualms I feel about these alternatives, and your job will be to establish the validity and compatibility of each of them.

      T. Confide your qualms, then, and I'll try and do as you ask.

3.00   S. Well, it seems to me that the premiss [1.11] to the effect that [a] literate is [a] man could be disproved thus:

3.101   No literate can be understood without literacy

3.102   Every man can be understood without literacy.

3.110   Again,

3.111   Every literate is susceptible of degree,

3.112   No man is susceptible of degree.

From either of these two sets of premises an identical conclusion can be drawn, namely:

3.113   No literate is [a] man.

3.20   T. It doesn't follow.

      S. Why not?

3.21   T. Does the name *animal* appear to you to signify anything besides animated sensitive substance?

      S. Certainly *animal* is just *animated sensitive substance,* and *animated sensitive substance* just *animal.*

      T. Quite so. And now tell me: is it not the case that every being which is just animated sensitive substance can be understood without rationality, and is not necessarily rational?

      S. I can't deny that.

      T. Hence every animal can be understood without rationality, and no animal is necessarily rational.

      S. There's no knowing what my admissions may not lead to, but I've a shrewd notion of what you're aiming at.

      T. On the other hand no man can be understood without rationality, and every man must necessarily be rational.

      S. Now I'm hemmed in on both flanks. For if I admit your last assertion, then you can infer that no man is animal; if, on the other hand, I deny it, you'll say that I'm not merely understandable without rationality, but that I am in fact completely devoid of it.

      T. Don't worry; the consequences aren't what you think they are.

      S. If that's a promise, then I freely grant any of your suggestions; otherwise I'm rather reluctant.

T. Then construct for yourself two syllogisms from these four premisses of mine.

S. They certainly can be laid out as follows:

3.221   Every animal can be understood without rationality

3.222   No man can be understood without rationality

Again:

3.231   No animal is necessarily rational

3.232   Every man is necessarily rational.

From this arrangement of the two sets of premisses it seems to follow in either case that

3.233   No man is animal.

This is altogether false, although there doesn't seem to be anything wrong with the foregoing premisses.

3.234   The two which have *man* as subject term [3.222, 3.232] are so self-evident that it would be silly to try to prove them, while the two which involve *animal* as subject term [3.221, 3.231] are apparently so sound that to deny them would be mere brashness. However, I notice that the structure of these two syllogisms is wholly similar to that of those two which I put forward a few moments ago [3.10, 3.11]. This makes me suspect that your only motive for producing them is to allow me to sort out the reasons for their obviously false conclusions that so I may realize that the same apply to the similar ones which I framed myself.

T. That is so.

S. Then show me how in both cases there can be so serious a mistake that although the premisses are true, and seem to be arranged in conformity with the rules of the syllogism, not the least scrap of truth emerges in their conclusions.

3.30   T. I'll do this for your syllogisms, and then you can analyse mine, if you like.

S. Do as you think fit.

3.310   T. Recall and reconstruct the syllogisms you produced before.

3.311   S. "Every man can be understood without literacy" [3.102].

T. What is it that you assert to be man and to be understandable without literacy?

S. Man.

T. Now include that which you understand within the
major premiss itself.

S. Every man can be understood to be man without literacy.

M. Agreed: now state the minor.

3.312   S. "No literate can be understood without literacy" [3.101].

T. What is it that cannot be understood to be literate
without literacy?

S. [A] literate.

T. State in full that which you understand, then.

S. No literate can be understood to be literate without
literacy.

3.3121   T. Now combine, as you did before, these two refor-
mulated premisses.

D.   Every man can be understood to be man without
literacy [3.311]

No literate can be understood to be literate without
literacy [3.312].

T. And now check whether they happen to have a common term; otherwise they are useless.

S. I can see that they involve no common term, so that
nothing follows from them.

T. Reconstruct your other syllogism [3.11].

3.320   S. You needn't bother to analyse it now. I see the fallacy.
I should have understood its premisses as if they asserted:

3.321   No man is susceptible of degree as man [3.112]

3.322   Every literate is susceptible of degree as literate
[3.111].

3.3221   And as these two propositions have no common term, they
prove nothing.

T. So it seems to you that nothing can be inferred from
your combination of premisses?

S. That certainly was my impression; but your question

makes me suspect that they perhaps still possess some concealed cogency. Yet how can they be used to prove something if they have no common term?

3.33   T.   It is not so much in the form of utterance as in its meaning that the common term of a syllogism is to be sought; for on the same grounds as those according to which no proof emerges from a mere verbal identity of terms without identical sense, there is nothing wrong with an identity which is understood although not made explicit. The meaning of the words is what really binds the syllogism together, and not just the words themselves.

3.40   S.   I'm waiting for you to restore cogency to my premisses.

     T.   You certainly can prove something from them, but not what you're looking for.

     S.   I'll be thankful for anything, whatever it is.

     T.   When it is asserted that

> Every man can be understood to be man without literacy [3.102,3.310]
> No literate can be understood to be literate without literacy [3.101,3.111],

doesn't this mean that

3.41   Being [a] man does not demand literacy, and

3.42   Being [a] literate demands literacy?

     S.   Quite so.

3.430   T.   And have these two premisses [3.41,3.42] which I asserted just now to be equivalent to the other two [3.310,3.311] a common term?

     S.   They have.

     T.   It follows, therefore, that

3.431   Being [a] literate is not being [a] man,

in the sense that

3.44   *literate* and *man* are not identically defined.

     S.   This is indubitably the case, as well as being logically sound.

3.450   T.   But it doesn't hence follow that

3.451   [a] literate is not [a] man [3.103, 3.113]
in your sense. If, however, you interpret
               [a] literate is not [a] man
as asserting:
3.452   [a] literate is not the same as [a] man
in the sense that they are not identically defined, then your conclusion is a true one.

3.500   S.   I understand your point.
         T.   If, then, you fully understand my point, tell me how
you would refute a syllogism composed as follows:
3.501   Every literate is asserted [to be] so in respect of
               quality;

3.502   No man is asserted [to be] so in respect of quality;

3.503   Hence: No man is literate.

3.510   S.   This seems to me to be like the assertion:

3.511   Every rational is asserted [to be] so in respect of
               quality,

3.512   No man is asserted [to be] so in respect of quality;

3.513   Hence: No man is rational.
But this is not capable of constituting a valid proof that *rational*
is predicable of no man.

3.520   Likewise that syllogism which you proposed just now
[3.50] doesn't necessarily prove that *literate* is not predicable
of man, for if we interpret them in such a way that their truth
is preserved, we see that its premisses amount to the following
assertions:

3.521   Every literate is asserted [to be] literate in respect
               of quality [3.501]

3.5220   No man is asserted [to be] man in respect of quality
               [3.502].

3.5221   But from these two propositions it by no means follows
         that

Literate is predicated of no man, for it is not the same term which is affirmed of *literate* and denied of *man*.

3.530   Of course, they would have a common term and be necessarily conclusive if *either*

3.531   The major remaining as it is [3.521]
the following minor were to be the case:

3.532   No man is asserted [to be] literate in respect of quality,

3.5330   *or*

3.5331   the minor remaining as before [3.5220]
the major could indeed become:

3.5332   Every literate is asserted to be man in respect of quality,

for then both these combinations [3.531,3.532; 3.5331, 3.5332] would produce the conclusion that

3.5333   *literate* is not predicable of any man.

3.540   For if one understands the assertion "[A] man is not [a] literate" [3.451] as though it amounted to "[A] man is not the same as [a] literate" in a sense similar to that found in the assertion, "Either the lightening is the flash or else the lightening is not the flash"—that is to say, "The lightening either is or else is not identical with the flash"—if, I say, one understands the assertion "[A] man is not [a] literate" in this sense, then it follows from the premises in question, on a careful scrutiny of their import, that

3.541   No man is literate.

3.542   This is because insofar as we are concerned to prove that

3.543   The essence of *man* is not the essence of *literate*
their meaning does involve a common term.

3.60   T. You have understood what I said alright, but perhaps you haven't scrutinised it properly.

        S. But how could I have understood it fully without having scrutinised it properly?

3.610   T. Tell me now: what would follow from the assertions:

3.611   No man can be understood without rationality,

3.612   Every stone can be understood without rationality?

S.   Hence,

3.6121   No stone is a man.

What else could follow?

3.620   T.   And what do you understand this to assert? Does
it mean

3.621   [A] stone is in no sense [a] man?

Or does it mean

3.622   [A] stone is not the same as [a] man?

S.   It means that [a] stone is in no sense [a] man.

3.630   T.   Tell me then: how does this last syllogism [3.61] differ
from that earlier one [3.10] of yours, in which you assert that [a]
literate cannot be understood without literacy, but [a] man can,
and hence [a] literate is not [a] man?

3.631   S.   As far as the logical cogency is concerned, I fail to
see any difference at all between the latter and the former; we
saw how the former [3.10] is to be understood as asserting that
          [a] literate cannot be understood to be [a] literate
                   without literacy [3.312], and that
          [a] man can be understood to be [a] man without
          literacy [3.311],
so that the latter [3.61] may likewise be understood to assert:

3.6311   [a] man cannot be understood to be [a] man
without rationality

3.6312   [a] stone can be understood to be [a] stone without
          rationality.

3.6313   Now the conclusion of the syllogism here in question
[3.6121] is securely established, since no stone is in any sense a
man [cf. 3.62]; hence it looks to me as though your skill in analysis
overwhelms the conclusion of that exactly similar syllogism of
mine [3.10]. So now I understand your saying that I had understood what you said, but without scrutinising it properly: I understood well enough what you might mean verbally, but I didn't
concentrate adequately on the exact point of what you were
meaning, since I had no idea how that syllogism might mislead
me.

3.6320   T. You certainly didn't concentrate adequately; what
you didn't realise was that way in which you might *not* have been
misled by it.

S. And what way is that?

T. It's true that if this syllogism which I put forward
just now [3.61] is expressed in the same way as in the analysis
[3.631] of your own [3.101, 3.102] which I gave, so that it asserts:

> No man can be understood to be [a] man without
> rationality [3.6311], and
>
> Every stone can be understood to be [a] stone
> without rationality [3.6312],

then it will be no more capable of producing a conclusion than
I asserted yours [3.101, 3.102] to be. Yet because the present one
[3.61] can be understood in another way—a way which is not
applicable to yours—it *does* produce the conclusion that [a]
stone can in no sense be [a] man [3.621]. For when I assert that

> No man can be understood without rationality
> [3.611],
>
> Every stone can be understood without rationality
> [3.612],

these propositions can, and indeed ought, to be taken to assert:

3.6321   No man is in some sense understandable without
                    rationality,

3.6322   Every stone is in any sense understandable without
                    rationality.

Whence it follows:

3.63221   No stone is in any sense a man.

3.6330   But your own premisses [3.10] are such that the truth
is not in the least susceptible of being likewise implicitly conveyed
by them; one cannot assert that

3.6331   No literate is in some sense understandable without
                    literacy [cf. 3.6321],

3.6332   Every man is in any sense understandable without
                    literacy, [cf. 3.6322]

for not only is it the case that

3.6333   Everything which is literate can be understood to

be [a] man without literacy [cf. 3.6331]
but also that

3.6334   No man can be understood to be [a] literate without literacy [cf. 3.6332].

3.6340   On this account your premisses cannot produce the conclusion:

3.6341   [a] literate is in no sense [a] man.

3.700   S.   I have no objection to raise against your verdict; but since you are guiding me surreptitiously, so that I don't rest content with understanding what you assert, but concentrate on exactly what it is that you are asserting, it now occurs to me that we should scrutinise the conclusion which you showed to follow from my syllogism [3.1], namely:

being [a] literate is not being [a] man [3.431].

3.701   If this [3.431] is granted, then whatever is essentially literate need not therefore be essentially man. But,

3.71   If *man* follows from *literate,* then the essence of man follows from the essence of literate.

3.711   But the second of these two conditionals doesn't hold [3.701], hence neither does the first, so that

3.7111   Not every literate is [a] man.

3.72   Further, every literate has some single feature which makes him susceptible of being [a] man, so that

Either every literate is [a] man, or none are.

3.721   But it has been shown [3.7111] that

Not every literate is [a] man,

therefore

3.7211   No literate is [a] man.

So now it looks as though you even more ingeniously yielded up for the taking that conclusion which you so cunningly lifted from my syllogism [3.10].

3.800   T.   Although it is quite true that I am surreptitiously leading you to concentrate on what you hear, it is nevertheless not my aim to give the process an air of complete futility. And now that you have gone and proved sophistically that no literate is a man [3.7211] by making use of the fact that being [a] literate is not being [a] man [3.431], it will nevertheless still be a handy exercise if you can get to the bottom of the fallacy which persists in muddling you with its apparent logicality.

S. Then show me just how and where this proof [3.7] involving *literate,* which I put together just now, is muddling me.

T. Let's go back to the cases of *animal* and *man*—cases in which we, as it were, so sense the truth that we can't be taken in by any invalid proof which might force us into a false opinion. Tell me: is not that which is involved in being a so-and-so expressible in a definition?

S. That is so.

T. Is the definition of *man* also the definition of *animal?*

3.8010   S. Not at all; for if *rational mortal animal,* the definition of *man,* were likewise the definition of *animal,* then to whatsoever *animal* was applicable, *rational mortal* would also apply;

3.8011   but this is not the case.

3.8012   T. Hence being [a] man is not being [an] animal.

S. So it follows.

3.810   T. Now from this conclusion, by using the same form of reasoning as that whereby a moment ago [3.7] you concluded that no literate is a man [3.7211], you can go on to show that

3.811   No man is [an] animal.

So if it's clear to you in this case that your form of reasoning leads to obvious untruth, you can have no confidence in the supposed truth [3.7211] which emerged from your earlier fiddling with the same form.

3.900   S. You've shown that it misled me; now show me just where it did do.

M. Don't you recall that a short while ago [3.4] I asserted, and you agreed, that

            Being [a] literate is not being [a] man [3.431]

means the same as

            The definition of *literate* is not the definition of *man* [3.44]?

This amounted to saying that

3.901   [A] literate and [a] man are not altogether identical [cf. 3.542] for just as *man* shouldn't be defined as possessing literacy, so also *literate* is not definable without literacy [cf. 3.41, 3.42].

3.910   Consequently that contention of yours [3.701] should be understood as follows:

3.911   If being literate is not being man and only man, then whatsoever is essentially literate need not on that account be essentially man and only man.

3.920   Likewise we are to understand that:

3.921   It is false that from *literate, man* and only *man* can be inferred, [cf. 3.71, 3.711],

that is to say:

3.922   If something is literate, then it does not follow that it is [a] man and only [a] man.

3.930   So that really the only conclusion is:

3.931   No literate is [a] man and only [a] man.

S.   Nothing could be more obvious.

3.940   T.   Were it to be proved true, as I believe could quite easily be done, that:

3.9410   Being [a] literate is not being [a] man

is like

3.9411   Being [a] white is not being [a] man

3.9412   (for [a] man can be without [a] white and [a] white can be without [a] man)

3.9420   then from this one could indeed draw the consequence that:

3.9421   Some literate can be other than [a] man.

S.   Why do we take all this trouble, then, if this can be proved? Prove it, and the question at issue will be settled.

3.9430   T.   That is an improper demand to make at this point, for in the present investigation we are not trying to find out whether it is *possible* for there to be some non-human literate, but whether

3.9431   there *is* some non-human literate.

And this, as you see, cannot be shown.

4.100   S. It's not yet obvious to me, for I still want to raise a
point to the contrary.

        T. Carry on.

        S. Aristotle showed that:

4.101   A literate is one of the things which are in a subject, but

4.102   No man is in a subject,
and from this it follows that

4.103   No literate is a man [cf. 1.11].

4.1100 T. Aristotle didn't want this consequence to be drawn
from what he said, for this same text of his uses *literate* not only
of such and such a man, but also of *man* and *animal.*

        S. How then can this syllogism of mine be refuted?

4.1101 T. Tell me now: when you speak to me about a literate,
whereof may I understand you to be speaking—of the name or
of the things signified by that name?

        S. Of the things signified.

        T. What things does it signify, then?

        S. *Man* and literacy.

4.1102 T. On hearing this name, then, I may understand *man*
or literacy, and

4.1103 when I speak of a literate, my speech may concern *man*
or literacy.

        S. That must be the case.

4.1104 T. Then tell me whether *man* is a substance, or in a subject.

        S. A substance, not in a subject.

4.1105 T. Is literacy a quality, and in a subject?

        S. It is both.

        T. Well then, nothing extraordinary is being said if
one asserts that

4.111   insofar as [a] man is concerned, [a] literate is a substance
and not in a subject, whereas

4.112   insofar as literacy is concerned, *literate* is a quality and in a
subject.

4.1200 S. I can't deny all this; but I might mention one more
reason why *literate* is not a substance:

4.1201   every substance is either primary or secondary, whereas *literate* is neither primary nor secondary substance.

T.   Call to mind that assertion of Aristotle's which I mentioned a little while ago [4.1100], according to which *literate* is both primary and secondary substance, since he invokes the fact that *literate* is used not only of such and such a man, but also of *man* and *animal*. On what grounds, then, can you show *literate* to be neither a primary nor a secondary substance?

4.121   S.   Because, unlike any substance, it is in a subject, also it is asserted of many things, and this is not a mark of primary substance.

4.122   Further it is neither genus nor species, nor is it asserted in respect of "whatness", as secondary substances are.

4.130   T.   None of your points, if you bear in mind what has been said, makes *literate* other than a substance.

4.131   For insofar as something literate is not in a subject, not only is it both genus and species, but it is also asserted in respect of "whatness"; this is because such a being is both man, i.e. a species, and animal, i.e. a genus, and these are asserted in respect of "whatness" [cf. 4.122].

4.132   Further, it is individual, like a man or an animal, for some literate is individual in the same way as are some man or some animal. For instance, Socrates is not only an animal and a man, but also a literate [cf. 4.121].

S.   There's no denying what you say.

4.14   T.   If you have no other grounds on which to base a proof that *literate* is not *man*, now prove that it's not literacy.

S.   I could manage to do that more easily by pointing than by argument, now that you have shattered all my contentions by showing the various meanings of literate, and how speech and understanding involving *literate* should correspond to those meanings [cf. 4.11]. Yet although I can't deny all this, my mind is nevertheless not satisfied in such a way that it, so to speak, can settle down, having discovered the required solution. Indeed, it looks to me as though you are concerned not so much with my enlightenment, as with the refutation of my points. But in fact my job was only to make explicit those factors which perplexed me when either of the alternatives in question was adopted [cf. 1.1, 1.2]; yours was either to refute one of these alternatives, or to show how both alternatives are mutually compatible.

T. Why, in your view, does not the fact that *literate* can be properly spoken of and understood sometimes in respect of *man* and sometimes in respect of literacy [4.11] sufficiently bring out the complete absence of incompatibility between the assertions that *literate* is a substance and that *literate* is a quality?

4.20 S. Because while it is quite true that no one who understands the name *literate* is unaware that it signifies literacy as well as *man*, yet if, on the strength of this, I were to assert at some gathering, "[A] literate is a useful form of knowledge", or, "That man displays an adequate literate", not only would this immensely irritate the literates: even the ignorant would guffaw.

4.210 So I just find it impossible to credit that authors of logical works can have no further grounds for so frequently and seriously committing themselves in writing in their books to positions that they would be ashamed to exemplify in conversation.

4.211 After all, in their logical discussions, when they want to show a quality or an accident, they most usually add "like *literate*", and so on.

4.212 Yet everyone's spoken usage vouches for the fact that *literate* is a substance rather than a quality or accident. But when they want to make a point about substance, they never suggest, "like *literate*", or anything of that sort.

4.22 The question boils down to this: if *literate*, because it signifies *man* and literacy, must therefore be said to be quality as well as substance, why is not *man* likewise quality as well as substance? After all, *man* signifies a substance along with all the characteristics of man, such as sensibility and mortality, yet when something is laid down in writing concerning some quality or other, we never find *man* produced as an example.

4.230 T. You reject my argument in favour of regarding *literate* as both substance and quality because it is not equally applicable to the case of the name *man*. You do this, I think, because you don't realize the vast difference between the way in which the name *man* signifies man's make-up, and the way in which the name *literate* signifies *man* and literacy.

4.231   We may take it that the name *man* signifies precisively, and as a single whole, the complete make-up of man. Of this, substance is the chief feature, as the ground and possessor of the others, and this not in the sense that it is incomplete without them, but rather that they are incomplete without it. After all, there is no characteristic of substance in the absence of which substance is also absent, whereas in the absence of substance no characteristics can exist. So that although all those characteristics, at the same time, form as it were a single whole covered by a single meaning, and receive as their appellation the single name *man*, nevertheless this name principally signifies and is appellative of substance; thus it would be correct to assert, "[The] substance is [a] man", and, "[The] man is [a] substance". Yet no-one would say, "[The] rationality is [a] man" or, "[The] man is rationality"; rather, [a] man is said to possess rationality.

4.232   On the other hand *literate* does not signify *man* and literacy as a single whole; precisively it signifies only literacy, and obliquely it signifies *man*.

4.233   Indeed, although the name *literate* is appellative of man, it nevertheless may not properly be said to signify *man*.

4.2340   Further, even though *literate* signifies literacy, it is not, however, appellative of literacy.

4.2341   Here I want to lay it down that the name of a thing is *appellative* of that thing when it is the name by which that thing is itself called in the customary course of utterance. Thus assertions such as "Literacy is literate", or "Literate is literacy" run counter to such customary usage; we say rather, "The man is literate", or, "The literate is a man".

4.240   S. I don't see the point of your saying that *literate* signifies literacy precisively and *man* obliquely, and yet that it only signifies literacy. For just as *man* comprises *animal* along with rationality and mortality, so that *man* signifies all three of these, so also, since a literate comprises man and literacy, the name *literate* must signify both of these; after all, neither a man without literacy nor literacy apart from a man are ever asserted to be literate.

T. Then if you are correct, "A man displaying literacy" would define and state what is involved in being a literate.

S. It can't be otherwise.

4.2411 T. Therefore, as literacy distinguishes the literate man from the illiterate, it is the literate's link with being—the feature of the literate which constitutes its being—the alternative presence and absence of which can only result in the literate's perishing.

S. And so what?

T. It would follow, then, that literacy is not an accident, but a constitutive characteristic, *man* being the genus, and *literate* the species. And the same would apply to the cases of whiteness and similar accidents. But the writings on the logical art as a whole show that this is not so.

S. Though I can't deny your assertions, I'm still not convinced that *literate* may not signify man.

4.2412 T. Let it be supposed that there is some rational animal— other than man—which displays literacy in the same way as does man.

S. That's easily supposed.

T. There is thus some non-man displaying literacy.

S. So it follows.

T. And every displayer of literacy is literate.

S. Granted.

T. There is therefore some literate non-man.

S. So it follows.

T. But you persist in asserting that *literate,* according to your understanding, comprises *man.*

S. I do.

T. So that some non-man is man; and this is false.

S. This is the outcome of the inference.

4.24121 T. So don't you see that *literate* no more signifies *man* than *white* does? It just happens to be the case that man alone displays literacy, whereas whiteness is found in beings other than men.

S.   That's what follows from the supposition adopted, but I'd rather you produced a proof which doesn't depend upon such supposititious cases.

4.2413   T.   In the same way as *animal* is not predicated along with *man*, since it is comprised in *man,* so also, if *man* is comprised in *literate,* the former is not simultaneously predicated along with the latter of some subject. For example, it is inappropriate to say that Socrates is an animal man.

S.   That can't be denied.

T.   But it is proper to say that Socrates is a literate man.

S.   It is proper.

T.   Therefore *man* is not comprised in *literate.*

S.   I grasp that it does so follow.

4.2414   T.   Again, if *literate* is *man displaying literacy,* then wherever *literate* appears the words *man displaying literacy* may be correctly substituted for it.

S.   That's right.

T.   Hence, if it is appropriate to say "Socrates is a literate man", it is equally appropriate to say, "Socrates is a man displaying literacy man".

S.   So it follows.

T.   But every man displaying literacy is a literate man.

S.   Yes.

T.   Thus Socrates, who is a man displaying literacy man, is a literate man man, and since a literate is a man displaying literacy, it follows that Socrates is a man displaying literacy man man, and so on to infinity.

S.   I can't gainsay such obvious inferences.

4.2415   T.   Again, if by *literate* we are to understand *man* as well as literacy, then in all cases of paronymous naming we must understand that which is named paronymously along with that from which it derives its name.

S.   That was my idea.

T.   So that *today's* must signify both that which is called *today's* and, in addition, it must signify *today.*

S.   And so what?

T. Thus *today's* signifies something having a temporal side-import.

S. It must be so.

T. Under such conditions, then, since *today's* is an incomplex expression having a temporal side-import, it must be a verb rather than a name.

4.30 S. You have proved to my satisfaction that *literate* does not signify *man*.

T. You see the point, then, of what I said about *literate* not signifying *man*? [4.233].

S. I do see it, and now I'm waiting for you to show that *literate* signifies literacy.

4.31 T. Didn't you assert a few moments ago [4.240] that *literate* signifies *man displaying literacy*?

S. That was my opinion.

T. But now it has been sufficiently proved that *literate* does not signify man?

S. Quite sufficiently.

T. What then is left?

S. *Displaying literacy* is all it can signify.

T. It signifies literacy, then.

4.40 S. It has been amply proved that

4.411 *literate* is appellative of man [4.233] and not of literacy [4.234], and

4.412 that it signifies literacy [4.232] but not *man* [4.233].

4.413 However, since you asserted that *literate* signifies literacy precisively and *man* obliquely [4.232], I'd like you to clear up the distinction between these two types of meaning so that I can understand how

4.414 *literate* doesn't signify that which it in some sense does signify, and

4.415 how *literate* can be an appellative of that which it doesn't signify.

4.4210 T. Suppose that, unknown to you, a white horse were enclosed in some building or other, and someone told you, "A white is in this building"—would that inform you that the horse was inside?

S.   No; for whether he speaks of a white, or of whiteness, or of that within which the whiteness is enclosed, no definite circumstance is brought to my mind apart from the essence of this colour.

T.   Even though you did happen to understand something over and above the colour, it is at least definite that the name in question conveys to you nothing as to exactly what that something is in which the colour is to be found.

4.4211   D.   That is quite definite. True, that name brings to mind a body or a surface, but this is simply because my experience has shown me that whiteness is usually found in such things: but of itself the name *white* signifies none of them, as was shown in the case of *literate*. And now I'm waiting for you to show me what it does in fact signify.

4.422   T.   Suppose you were to see a white horse and a black bull standing together, and someone gave the order, "Give it a thwack!", thereby meaning the horse, but without giving any indication as to which he intended: would you then know that he was referring to the horse?

S.   No.

T.   But suppose, while still in ignorance, you were to ask "Which?", and he were to reply, "[The] white!", would you then gather his reference?

S.   I would gather from the name *white* that he meant the horse.

T.   Thus for you the name *white* would signify the horse.

S.   It certainly would.

T.   And do you notice that this would be in a fashion other than that proper to the name *horse?*

4.4231   S.   I quite see that. I notice that even before I know the horse to be white, the name *horse* signifies to me the substance *horse* precivisely, not obliquely.

4.4232   On the other hand, the name *white* signifies the substance *horse* not precisely, but only obliquely, that is, thanks to my being aware that the horse is white.

4.4233 Now the name *white* is equisignificant with the phrase *having whiteness;* similarly, the precise effect of this phrase is to bring to my mind the understanding of whiteness, but not of the thing which has the whiteness, so that the word *white* has the same effect.

4.4234 However, because I know, otherwise than by means of the name *white*—by sight, for example—that the whiteness is in the horse, when whiteness has been thus conveyed by means of that word, I also gather the reference to the horse because I know that the whiteness is in the horse. Nevertheless this is otherwise than by means of the name *white,* even though that word is an appellative of the horse.

4.424 T. So now you grasp how *white* does not signify what it does in someway signify [4.414] and how it is appellative of what it does not signify? [4.415]

S. I now see this further point: *white* signifies yet doesn't signify the horse;

4.4241 it signifies the horse obliquely, and not precisively, and nevertheless *white* is an appellative of the horse.

4.4242 Further, I realize that what I now discern in the case of *white* is applicable to *literate* and all like paronyms.

4.4243 On these grounds it appears to me that the signification of both names and verbs can be diversely classified: one sort is precisive signification, and the other sort is oblique.

4.430 T. Notice also that while the precisive type of signification pertains essentially to significant utterance as such, the other type is only accidental to such utterance.

4.431 Thus, when a noun or a verb is defined as a *significant utterance,* the signification in question is to be understood only as being of the precisive sort. Were the oblique sense of *signification* to be understood in the definition of a noun or a verb, then *today's* would be a verb, not a noun, for it sometimes signifies something having a temporal side-import, and this, as I remarked before [4.2415] is proper to a verb, not to a noun.

4.500 S. Obviously, it is as you say.

4.501 Nevertheless it is awkward to think of *literate,* although it signifies literacy, as being a quality,

4.5020   or to think of man alone, that is, without literacy, as being literate;

4.5021   for since man can only be literate alone or with literacy, that man alone is literate follows as a consequence of the proof [4.24] that man along with literacy is not literate.

4.5022   And although the name *literate* signifies literacy, nevertheless the correct answer to the question " What is literate?" could scarcely be "*Literate* is literacy" or, "*Literate* is a quality".

4.503   And again, since a literate must participate in literacy, it follows that a man can only be a literate in conjunction with literacy.

4.510   T.   The assertion that man alone, in the sense of man without literacy, is literate, can be interpreted in two fashions, one correct, the other incorrect, and this is enough to solve your problem.

4.511   On the one hand man alone, without literacy, is indeed literate, for he alone ever possesses literacy; literacy itself does not possess literacy, either alone or along with man.

4.5120   On the other hand man alone, deprived of literacy, is not literate, for in the absence of literacy no one can be literate.

4.5121   The first case is like that of someone preceding, leading someone else, and alone being the one who precedes, for one who follows is not a precedent, either separately or in such a way that the two form a single precedent. In the second case, one who is alone is not one who precedes, for unless there is a follower, it is impossible for there to be a precedent.

4.5122   And of course, when it is asserted that *literate* is a quality, this assertion is only correct if made in the sense which occurs in Aristotle's treatise *On the Categories*.

4.513   S.   But doesn't that treatise make the point, "Everything which is, is one or other of either substance or quantity or quality", and so on? So if *man* alone is literate, a substance alone is literate. How comes it then that that treatise accounts *literate* a quality rather than a substance?

4.5141　T.　Although the text in question might be interpreted in the way you claim, for everything which is is some one or other of the things you mention, nevertheless Aristotle's main intention in that book was not to show this, but rather to show how every name or verb *signifies* one or other of them.

4.5142　It was not his aim to show the nature of individual circumstances, nor yet of what circumstances individual words are appellative; rather he wished to show what circumstances they signify.

4.5143　However, since words only signify circumstances, he had, in order to indicate what words signify, to indicate what those circumstances might be.

4.5144　For, without going into further detail, the classification which he undertook at the opening of his work on the Categories is enough to bear out what I assert. He does not say, "Each item of whatever is is either a substance or a quantity", and so on, nor yet, "Each item of whatever is expressed in an incomplex fashion has 'substance' or 'quality' as its appellation", but rather, "Each item of whatever is expressed in an incomplex fashion *signifies* a substance or a quality".

　　　　S.　Your point is persuasive.

4.515　T.　Now when Aristotle says, "Each item of whatever is expressed in an incomplex fashion signifies a substance or a quantity", and so on, to which type of signification does it appear to you that he is referring—to that whereby the utterances as such signify precisively, and which pertains to them essentially, or to that other type which is oblique and only accidental to the utterances?

　　　　S.　He can only be referring to that sort of signification whereby they signify precisively, and which he himself imputes to such utterances when defining the noun and the verb.

　　　　T.　And do you consider that anywhere in his work he treated the matter otherwise than he did in this classification, or that any of his followers wished to adopt an attitude differing from his on this topic, when writing on logic?

　　　　S.　Their writings contain no grounds whatsoever for

such an opinion, for at no point does one find any of them prof-
fering an utterance to show something it can signify obliquely;
they always proffer an utterance to show what it signifies precisively. Thus, when they want to show a substance, none of them
proffers *white* or *literate*; however, *white* and *literate*, and so on,
are advanced as examples when they are dealing with quality.

4.600   T.   So that if, given the aforementioned classification, I
were to ask you what *literate* is in terms of that classification, and
in keeping with the opinions of those whose logical writings make
appeal to it, what kind of a question would I be asking, and
what kind of a reply would you give?

4.601   S.   This question must concern either the word or the
circumstance it signifies. Hence, since it is agreed that in terms
of this distinction *literate* signifies literacy and not man, I would
reply immediately:

4.602   if your question concerns the word, then it is a word
signifying quality;

4.603   if, however, your question is about the circumstance, then
it *is* a quality.

4.604   T.   You realise, do you not, that in this same text Aristotle
refers to words by the name of the circumstance which those
words signify, and not by the name of those of which they are
merely appellative? Thus, when he says, "Every substance seems
to signify this particular thing", what he means is, "Every word
signifying a substance". It is in this way that he names, or rather
shows circumstances—as you reminded us just now—by recourse to utterances which only signify them, and which frequently are not appellative of them at all.

4.610   S.   I can't help realising this. Hence, whether the question
is posed in respect of the word or in respect of the circumstance,
when one asks what *literate* is according to the treatise of Aristotle, and according to his followers, the correct answer is: a
quality.

4.611   However, from the point of view of appellation it certainly
is a substance.

4.620   T.   Quite so: we mustn't be disturbed by the fact that logicians make written assertions about words insofar as they signify, and yet, in speaking, given the appellative function of those words, use them in a fashion which is at variance with those assertions, any more than we are when the grammarians assert one thing about a word considered as an exemplar, but quite another when it is considered in relation to the constitution of circumstances.

4.621   After all, they tell us that "stone" is masculine in gender, "rock" feminine, but "property" neuter, and that "to fear" is an active verb, whereas "to be feared" is passive; yet no one asserts that a stone is masculine, a rock feminine, or property neither masculine nor feminine, nor that to fear is to perform an action, whereas to be feared is to undergo an action.

4.700   S.   Clearly it would be unreasonable of me to question what you have laid down, but there is still another point in connection with this problem which I would like you to clear up for me. Thus, if *literate* is a quality because it signifies a quality, I fail to see why *accoutred* is not a substance since it signifies substance; or if accoutred is in the category of "having" because it signifies a having, I don't see why *literate* should not be in that same category, since it too signifies a having. This is because in exactly the same way as *literate* is proved to signify a quality because it signifies having a quality, so also *accoutred* should signify a substance since it signifies having substance, namely accoutrements. Likewise, since *accoutred* quite obviously signifies having (for it signifies *having* accoutrements), *literate* must also signify having, since it signifies *having* learning.

S.   T.   If we are to take these points into consideration I just can't deny that *accoutred* is substance or *literate* a having.

S.   Can a single circumstance be assigned to different categories, then? I would like you to settle this point for me.

4.710   T.   I do *not* think that any one and the same circumstance can properly be assigned to several categories, although in certain cases this may be a mere matter of opinion; my own view is that this calls for a rather more lengthy discussion than we bargained for in our present brief argument. However, I do not see why one word signifying several things, but not as a single whole, should not at times be variously categorised, as when *white* is said to be both a quality and a having. In this case *white* does not signify quality and having as a single whole in the way that *man* does signify as a single whole both the substance and the qualities which constitute man. This is because that which receives the appellation *man* is one thing constituted in the way I mentioned, whereas the thing that receives the appellation *white* is not just some one thing comprising a having and a quality, for only the thing that has whiteness receives the appellation *white,* and such a thing is certainly not composed of a having and a quality.

4.711   In contrast, should it be asserted both that *man* is a substance and *man* is a quality, then one and the same thing which this name signifies, and of which it is appellative, would be asserted to be both a substance and a quality, and this seems unacceptable.

4.712   When, however, we say that *white* is both a quality and a having, we are *not* asserting that that of which this name is appellative is a quality and a having, but that this name signifies both, and nothing improper follows.

4.713   S.   But why then is not *man* a substance and a quality in terms of Aristotle's classification, on account of its signifying both, in the same way as *white* is a quality and a having on account of its signifying both?

4.714   T.   I think that what I've already said should be enough to settle your query: *man* predominantly signifies substance—the whole that it signifies *is* a substance, something qualified, rather than a quality. On the other hand *white* has no dominant signification but relates equally to quality and having, nor does any kind of unity result from white's predominantly signifying one or other of these.

4.72   S.   Do you mind explaining more fully how it comes

about that something forming a single whole does not result from the things signified by *white?*

T. If some thing is composed of them, then it is either a substance or something in some one or other of the categories.

S. It must be so.

T. But no category comprises both having and whiteness.

S. I can't deny that.

T. Again, a single whole can only be made up out of a multiplicity either by the composition of parts which are of the same category, in the way that *animal* is made up of body and soul, or by the assemblage of a genus and one or more characteristics, as in the cases of *body* and *man*, or by the species and collection of properties, as with Plato. Now the things that *white* signifies do not belong to one category only, neither is one of them related to the other either as genus to constitutive characteristic or as species to collection of properties, nor yet again are they characteristics pertaining to one genus; they are in fact accidents of the same subject: yet *white* does not signify that subject—it signifies only a having and a quality. Therefore no unity results from the things that *white* signifies.

4.800 S. Your assertion seems to me to be perfectly reasonable; still, I would like to hear what you would reply should someone object as follows to what you said about *white* signifying only a having and a quality:

4.801 as *white* is equivalent to having whiteness, it does not determinately signify this or that thing having whiteness, such as a body; rather it signifies indeterminately some thing having whiteness.

4.8020 This is because a white is either that which has whiteness or that which has not whiteness; but that which has not whiteness is not white, so that a white is that which has whiteness. Further, since everything which has whiteness must needs be something, a white must be something which has whiteness, or something having whiteness.

4.8021 Finally, *white* signifies either something having whiteness or nothing; but nothing cannot be conceived to have whiteness, hence *white* must signify something having whiteness.

4.810   T.   The question is not whether everything which is white is something, or whether it is that which has, but whether the word *white* contains in its signification the expression *something*, or *that which has,* in the way that *man* contains *animal,* with the consequence that in the same way as *man* is *rational mortal animal,* so also *white* is *something having whiteness* or *that which has whiteness.*

4.811   Now many things are necessary to the being of anything you care to mention, and yet are not signified by the name of the thing in question. For example, every animal must be coloured as well as either rational or irrational, yet the name *animal* signifies none of these things. Hence, although there is no white which is not something having whiteness or that which has whiteness, nevertheless *white* need not signify these facts.

4.8120   Nevertheless, let us suppose that *white* can signify *something having whiteness.* Now *something having whiteness* is the same as *something white.*

S.   It must be so.

T.   *White* therefore always signifies *something white.*

S.   Quite so.

T.   So that wherever *white* appears it is always correct to substitute *something white* for *white.*

S.   That follows.

T.   Hence when *something white* is used, the double expression *something something white* is also correct; when the double is correct, so also is the triple, and so on to infinity.

S.   This is a derivable absurdity.

4.8121   T.   Again, let *white* be also identical with *that which has whiteness.* Now *has* is the same as *is having.*

S.   It can't be otherwise.

T.   Therefore *white* is the same as *that which is having whiteness.*

S.   Exactly.

T.   But when *having whiteness* is used, this phrase is equisignificant with *white.*

S. That is so.

T. Hence *white* is the same as *that which is white.*

S. So it follows.

T. Wherever, therefore, *white* appears, *that which is white* may properly be substituted for it.

S. That I can't deny.

T. Then if *white* is the same as *that which is white,* it is also the same as *that which is that which is white;* if this is the case, so also is *that which is that which is that which is white,* and so on to infinity.

S. This is just as logical and just as absurd as that case in which the repetition of *something something* . . . results.

4.813 T. And now, when it is asserted that *white* signifies either something having whiteness or nothing, and this is interpreted as asserting that *white* signifies either *something having* or *not-something having,* then as *not-something* is an infinite name, this disjunction is neither complete nor true, and hence proves nothing. It's like asserting, "The blind man either sees something or he sees not-something". If, on the other hand, the assertion is interpreted as meaning that the word either signifies or does not signify *something having,* the disjunction is complete and true, and is not incompatible with what has been laid down previously.

4.82 S. It's sufficiently obvious that *white* signifies neither *something having whiteness* nor *that which has whiteness,* but only *having whiteness,* that is, a quality and a having, and as these alone do not constitute one thing, *white* is both of them, since it signifies both equally. I see that this reasoning is valid in relation to whatever is expressed in an incomplex fashion, and which likewise signifies some multiplicity which is of such a kind as does not form a single whole. It also seems to me that no valid objection can be made to the theses you have advanced in the course of this discussion.

4.83 T. So it seems to be at the present moment. However, you are well aware of the extent to which our contemporary logicians are at loggerheads about this problem of yours, so I don't want you to stick to our findings to the length of stubbornly hanging on to them should someone manage, by the use of better opposing arguments, to demolish our results and establish different ones. Should this occur, at least you can't deny that all this has been handy as an exercise in discussion.

IV

THE PROBLEM OF PARONYMS

§4.01   Now follows an attempt to site the dialogue *De grammatico* within its context of linguistic and logical discussion, and to suggest why *"grammaticus"* came to be chosen as an example, as well as to illustrate its aptness. It will then become incidentally evident that the lack of understanding which has previously been the lot of this work may in part be traced to the remarkable fact that its example-word, and hence its title, have never been given a satisfactory translation into the modern languages of Western Europe. This is, in fact, not the main reason for the failure of appreciation: sheer blindness to the point at issue has been another (§5.31). The terms of the original discussion will for the most part still be used without any detailed elucidation of their semantical status; this must be so, since otherwise, as Anselm himself shows, the problems raised tend to disappear; it is within the meaning of sentences involving such terms that the questions really have their roots. Assessments, informal and formal, of the status of the dialogue's discourse, will be presented in §5 and §6.

§4.1   *Paronyms in Ancient Logic and Grammar*

§4.101   The dialogue takes its customary title from its *incipit*,

viz: "*De grammatico . . .*", and from the fact that "*grammaticus*"
is employed as a crucial example. However, as its first sentence also
makes clear that this word is used as an instance of a paronym
(*nomen denominativum,* denominative name) from which general-
isations are permissible, a more suitable translation of its title would
be "Dialogue on Paronyms".

§4.102   The last notable use in English logical literate of the term
"denominative" is one which occurs in J. S. Mill's logic (*MSL* I,
Ch. II, §5), and is enlarged on below (§4.103, §4.3); the tradition of
its use extends back to the ancient grammarians and logicians.
Priscian employs the term to cover any kind of derivation from
a *nomen,* or name; as "*nomen*" is for the ancient Latinists a wider
term than the modern "noun" (it embraces what would nowadays
be distinguished as adjectives) a very wide range of words is here
in question. Of course, the notion of derivation need not be taken
too seriously here: usually some species of word-similarity is in
question. The same applies to the cases envisaged by Aristotle in
Ch. I of his *Categoriae*: things are there stated to be named paronymously (or derivatively) "which derive their name from some other
name, but differ from it in termination. Thus the literate derives
his name from 'literacy', and the courageous from 'courage'". However, Boethius, when commenting on this passage (*B*167D), appears
to restrict his account to contexts of the elementary sort which are
indicated by Aristotle's concrete examples, and asserts that the
(supposed) derivation of the *nomen* reflects "participation" in whatever is named by the cognate abstract noun; e.g. because a given
man participates in the virtue of justice, we denominate him "just"
(*B*168A). This Platonic-sounding supplement does not necessarily
have the consequence that those who make use of the term "paronym" (or "denominative name") are committed to holding that
we first perceive, e.g. the quality, subsequently note the participant,
and finally consider ourselves licensed to use paronyms in respect of
that participant. Boethius remarks that the opposite is the case:
whites and literates are cognitively prior ("*notior*") to whiteness
and literacy respectively (*B*240C). In all, he holds, three marks
distinguish the paronymous situation: (i) "participation" in some-

thing by the thing paronymously named, (ii) participation by the paronym in the name of that "something" mentioned in (i), i.e. the two names must differ in termination only, and (iii) the non-identity of the paronym and the name of that in which the thing parony-mously named participates (*B*168A; cf. *HSL*2.22, *HSL*3.01). When condition (iii) is unfulfilled, says Boethius, equivocation results. Thus *"musica"* names both a female musician and the art in which she is versed (*B*168B-C). Leaving aside this third condition, at least three variable factors are apparent here, and thinkers of the Middle Ages were quick to exploit them. The first such variable is the notion of "participation" used in respect of things. Now while derivative *words* may be said to "participate" in the words from which they are derived, or which have the same stem, and this in a perfectly familiar and straightforward manner, nevertheless the use of "participate" in respect of *things* is far from intelligible. In practice this was later, e.g. at the hands of Aquinas, to be interpreted as any kind of connection implied by the purposive transference of words in accordance with human needs and interests. The second variable lies in the range of objects in which such partici-pation is envisaged. Boethius' examples appear to confine this range to qualities in which things might be said to "participate in com-mon". But there seems to be no reason why this range should not be extended to other categories (quantity, state, etc.). A most serious question here still remains to be faced, nevertheless, namely: what kind of thing *is* a quality, if it really is a thing at all? The third variable lies in the language used. Thus, suppose participation in qualities is in question: exactly what is to count as a paronym will then depend either upon the extent to which names given to things on account of their qualities happen to have, in the language of the period, corresponding abstract names of those qualities, or *vice versa* upon the extent to which abstract names of qualities happen to have corresponding paronyms. A simple example of the effect of this third variable can be drawn from Boethius' own text: *"virtus"* is the name of a quality to which, it would appear, the Latin of Boethius' time had no corresponding paronym, since he tells us that a man having *virtus* was called *"sapiens"* (wise) or *"probus"* (honest) (*B*254B); "*virtus*" could hence not be considered by him in connection with paronyms. Yet in medieval Latin the corresponding paronym ("*virtuosus*") exists and is used freely.

§4.103   In a situation of the kind described, at least two reactions are possible: one can either recognise that there are limits to the use of linguistic classifications for the delineation of logical problems, or one can make artificial additions to the language in an attempt to ensure that it reflects those problems. Aristotle, on whose text Boethius comments, is quite alive to the dangers of circumscribing a class of cases by reference to the contingent features of non-technical language, and hence takes the first course: he merely uses paronymy as a rough guide, and concludes by noting that the name borne by a thing in virtue of a quality possessed by that thing may or may not be derivative from the name of that quality (*AC* 10^{b}9). Boethius, in somewhat the same spirit, used the general heading "*qualia*" for things having qualities, whether paronymously named or no (*B*253B). The medievals, following a suggestion made by Boethius (*B*463-464), but not extensively exploited by him, tended to take the second course, and invented constructions to fit their needs: this is particularly evident in the case of abstract nouns like "*animalitas*", "*corporeitas*", and the like, against which Locke inveighs (*LE*III Ch.8, §2), although they are no worse than the abstract nouns formed by the addition of "-ness", "-hood" or "-ity" to the concrete noun, and used in contemporary philosophical and logical writings in English. However, this possibility of systematic artificial amendment of natural language can, unless used with great caution, give the impression that all cases which are thus rendered linguistically alike are susceptible of like logical classification. The difference between the cautious and incautious attitude on this point may be exemplified by the cases of Aquinas and J.S. Mill: both hold explicitly that "white" and "man" are paronymous: in Aquinas' terms, "things are ordinarily denominated from their forms, as the white from 'whiteness' and man (*homo*) from 'humanity' (*humanitas*)" (*AST*I q. 37, art 2, c.); in a similar vein Mill asserts, "Snow, and other objects, receive the name 'white' because they possess the attribute which is called 'whiteness'; Peter, James, and others, receive the name 'man' because they possess the attributes which are considered to constitute humanity. The attribute, or attributes, may therefore be said to denominate those objects, or to give them a common name" (*MSLi*, Ch.2, §5). Now this is part of Mill's evidence for the possibility of treating both "man" and "white" as belonging to the class of "connotative" names, and so of regarding them as signifying in the same fashion. Aquinas, on the other hand, was not tempted in this way, as an inspection of his commentary on the *Posterior Analytics* makes clear (*APA*285, 295; cf. *APA*87, 259, 281, 289).

§4.104 Boethius' description of paronymy not only contains the variables which have been mentioned, but is also such that any change in the interpretation of one of those variables tends to affect the interpretation of the others: thus it would appear that the meaning of paronyms such as "sweet" or "white" is bound up in some sense with the corresponding qualities ("sweetness", "whiteness"), hence such denominatives were said to "signify a quality" (*Nihil enim "album" significat quam qualitatem*, B194C; cf. *AC*3ᵃ 18). Now given the use of "*humanitas*" in medieval Latin to mean "human nature", and granted that "white" signifies the quality whiteness, are we to say also that "*homo*" likewise signifies the quality *humanitas?* Hence arise repercussions in the range of the second variable: is *humanitas* a quality in which men participate—a set of attributes, a form, a nature, or a "quiddity"? And leaving aside the vexed question of the ontological status of attributes, one can still ask: if "man" signifies, say, a quality in this way, does this not exclude the view that man is a substance, as opposed to a quality? In Minto's words: "When we say 'This is a man' do we not declare what sort of a thing he is? Do we not declare his Quality? If Aristotle had gone further along this line, he would have arrived at the modern point of view [i.e. Mill's] that a man is a man in virtue of his possessing certain attributes, that general names are applied in virtue of their connotation" (*MID*117). Minto goes on to suggest, most significantly, that Aristotle failed to take this further step, which would make "man" into a quality-signifying word, only because he had not at his disposal a "separate name in common speech for the common attributes of man" (*MID*118). Boethius, when commenting on the topic of "secondary substances" appears to go quite a long way in the direction suggested by Minto, when he admits that "man" "shows what a substance is like", i.e. shows its qualities (*B*194). Indeed, he holds that both "man" and "white" signify qualities in ways sufficiently similar to establish the need for further criteria to distinguish which of the two indicates a "substance", e.g. lack of contrary, insusceptibility of degree, and so forth (*B*195C *et seq.*).

§4.105   Very little effort is required in order to imagine the various complex aspects of actual linguistic practice which the notion of paronymy can be assumed to cover when the variable possibilities of the Boethian delineation are exploited to the full. Aquinas, prompted by Aristotle's *Metaphysica,* recognises that anything connected with anything else, in any one of numberless fashions, can be said to be named paronymously ("denominated") from that "something else". How diverse these fashions are may be gathered from many examples, e.g. "From the health that is in the animal, not only is the animal, which is the subject of the health, denominated healthy, but the medicine is also asserted to be so, since it is the cause of that health, likewise the diet, insofar as it preserves it, and the urine, inasmuch as it is a sign thereof" (*ASTIII*, q.60, art.1, c.). This passage starts off with the simple "quality" case of the same sort as Aristotle's example in the *Categoriae,* and both this and the extensions thereof each correspond to various interests and points of view: that of the man (animal) who is healthy, as well as the doctor's, the dietetist's and the uroscopist's. From this and other cases cited by St. Thomas, usually following Aristotle, it is clear that for him paronyms might be said to exemplify that feature of the so-called "natural" languages which has been called "open texture" by Waissman (cf. *MC*174).

§4.106   In Aquinas too is to be found the distinction which is suggested by the elaborations described, namely that between extrinsic and intrinsic paronymy. As the terms imply, the extrinsic sort is found when that from which the thing receives its name is somehow external to that thing, e.g. when "the located" is so called from "location", and "the measured" from "measure" (*ASTI*, q.6, art.4 c.). In contrast, the cases in which qualities are possessed by the object itself, as in the simple examples given in the *Categoriae*, constitute intrinsic paronymy. One of the ways in which this distinction passed into modern philosophy may be seen in the Logic of Port Royal, where internal and external *modes* are described (*LP*37-38). Ockham distinguishes, yet again, between two types of paronymy which can be gathered from Aristotle's original text: "A paronymous term can for the present be taken in two senses. If it is taken strictly, a paronymous term is one which begins as the abstract term does, but does not have the same ending, and signifies an accident, e.g. from 'bravery' we have the paronymous term 'brave', or from 'justice', 'just'. Taken broadly, however, a paronymous term is one which has the same beginning as the abstract term and does not have the same ending; but it does not matter whether it signifies an accident or not. As, for instance, from 'life' something is said to be 'living' " (*OPW*71-2).

§4.107 Now although Anselm is, in *De grammatico*, concerned primarily with what Ockham would call "strict" and Aquinas "intrinsic" paronymy, he does there suggest and imply certain extensions (4.42, 4.43). And in yet another work (*SNUW*34.29.39) he makes a very wide generalisation which, in terms of his general theory that a word may be used either in its strict sense (*proprie*) or in a non-strict sense (*non proprie*) lays down principles covering all the cases later adopted by Aquinas (cf. *HG*). In any case, the notion of intrinsic paronymy in respect of a quality which is so prominent in *De grammatico*, is in fact a means to a further and more important end. It is evident that, impressed by the linguistic fact recorded by Locke, viz: "as to our ideas of substances, we have few or no abstract names at all" (*LE*III, Ch.8, §2), Anselm is relying on this sort of paronymy to exclude those concrete nouns which name what he would call substances. He did not have at his disposal the whole of the battery of abstract names which, as Locke points out, "the schools have introduced" (*"animalitas", "humanitas"* as the correlate of *"homo", "corporeitas"*) or have "but timorously

ventured on" ("*aureitas*", "*saxeitas*", "*ligneitas*", and so forth) and
which would have brought the corresponding concrete nouns ("*animal*" etc.) into the field of the paronymous situation. Anselm is in
fact in a position somewhat more akin to that of the modern non-phil-
osophical user of English, whose feelings are voiced by Locke, than
to that of the later and larger-vocabularied scholastics. For such a
user, what may loosely be called the names of substances have,
as Locke points out, no corresponding abstract names, and the
invention of these by the addition of "-ness" or "-hood" smacks
not a little of artificiality ("tree"-"treeness"). In contrast, each adjective usually already possesses its natural abstract correlate.
Nevertheless, there does exist in English an interesting class of
abstract nouns, nearly all of which purport to name a quality or
state associated with human beings alone, and which have as correlates not adjectives, but words classified by grammarians as concrete nouns, e.g. "rascality"-"rascal", "captaincy"-"captain", "re-
gency"-"regent" etc. Correspondingly, there exists in Latin the
class of those adjectives, each with its cognate abstract noun, which
happen *as a matter of fact* to apply intrinsically to human beings
alone: of these "*grammaticus*", the example used in *De grammatico*,
is one. Since, for the ancient grammarians, any Latin adjective was
a form of *nomen* (or name), and was inflected like a noun as well
as being used quite naturally in a nominal sense, the two classes of
words—the English and the Latin—are very much akin, and raise
the same kind of problem: is their meaning substantive (since they
are names and always have to do with human beings) or merely
adjectival (as indicated by the existence of their corresponding
abstract nouns)? That this difficulty is already evident in Priscian
will be shown below, and it is noteworthy that the terms concerning
which recent traditional logicians debated as to whether they
should be classified as "concrete" or "attributive", although not
always strictly paronyms, nevertheless for the most part belong
precisely to this type of case, e.g. "artist", "traitor", "father", and
"musician" in H.W.B. Joseph's logic (*JL*155, note 1, *JL*37, note 1).
But once the problem has been posed thus in respect of the restricted
class of concrete nouns of the sort mentioned (in English) and

adjectives of the corresponding sort (in Latin), there seems little cause not to expand it to embrace Latin adjectives as a whole (in view of their grammatically nominal uses) and likewise to all English adjectives, when it is recalled that these become nouns on the assumption of noun-inflection, or are used as nouns when they have an article attached. To sum up: the narrower use of the term "paronym" which is the minimum required to make the problem of *De grammatico* intelligible, comprises in English almost any concrete noun having not too artificial an abstract correlate, and all adjectives, bearing in mind the possible nominal functions of the latter. The concrete noun "man", in spite of the present existence of "manhood" or "humanity", is assumed to be excluded from the class of paronyms, since "*homo*" is used by Anselm as a stock example of a non-paronymous name. He was certainly familiar with the logical use of "*humanitas*" to refer to whatever is involved in being a human being: this use occurs throughout Boethius' translations and commentaries (e.g. *BCP*85B, *BCP*93D, *BCP*121B, *BCP*-150B, *BCP*150D, *BC*271D, *BDIG*322D, *BDIG*463A, *BTC*1119A, *BTC*1121C). Anselm makes use of "*humanitas*" in the sense in *Epistola de Incarnatione Verbi,* and would doubtless regard "*humanus*" as the cognate paronym (*S*II26). This logical sense of "*humanitas*" is of course to be distinguished from that other sense which occurs in earlier Latin (cf. *PH*), and which is akin to the alternative modern sense. Fundamentally, therefore, we are faced with a highly unsatisfactory delimitation of a sphere of logical interest: it reflects the state of philosophical Latin in Anselm's time, and thereby illuminates the temporary nature of a classification so dependent on contingent linguistic factors.

§4.108   Yet notwithstanding the ease with which reasons for deprecating Anselm's use of the notion of paronymy may be found, there are at least two redeeming points which should not be overlooked. In the first place, as soon as one ceases to view a "natural" language as a pure datum, and in abstraction from the purposes for which human beings employ it, the air of blind contingency which attaches to the notion of paronymy tends to be somewhat dissipated. There are plenty of pre-philosophical occasions on which one wishes to compare one thing or person with another in respect of some quality, and hence there exists a natural tendency for there to be a name for that quality (cf. B255-6). Further, when names imposed on account of states are counted as paronyms (since one has "fatherhood"-"father", "pregnancy"-"pregnant", and so on) it is also clear that occasions for the use of the corresponding abstract nouns do in fact often arise: we frequently desire to place, date or measure the beginning, end, or duration of a state. Yet no such occasions can be envisaged for the use of the abstract nouns corresponding to such concrete names as "man", "dog", and "tree", for example; not only are the objects named by these names not suspectible of degree in respect of the qualities apparently named by such abstract nouns as "manhood" (or "humanity"), "dogness", or "treeness", but also the duration of the quality is here coterminous with the existence of the object which has it. It is not surprising, therefore, that such abstract nouns belong only to that relatively artificial stratum of language which owes its existence to philosophy or logic. The pre-philosophical paronym with which *De grammatico* is primarily concerned, the paronym in Ockham's strict sense, which "signifies an accident", will always in the concrete embody news: the philosopher's artificial paronym will tend to occur only in the course of his important truisms. Secondly, the main weight of Anselm's discussion scarcely depends on the classification of words as paronyms; for the most part he merely contrasts a case ("man") which in some sense can be said to "signify a substance" with cases like "white" and "literate" which for him differ from "man" in being paronymous. Having shown that the examples do not all perform their significatory functions in the same way, he generalises on the distinctions thus illuminated. Such generalisation can still remain effective when "*homo*" has become, as it has by Aquinas' time, the cognate paronym of "*humanitas*", and so entered linguistically into the class of words from which Anselm hoped to distinguish it.

§4.109   Centuries before Anselm, Priscian had been faced with what was, at least verbally, the same question, and in attempting to provide some criterion whereby quality-indicating words could be distinguished from substance-indicating words, only bequeathed confusion to posterity by his choice of example. It has been pointed out how English adjectives are the closest modern approximation to the bulk of the paronyms recognised by Anselm, and concerning *adiectiva*, themselves a species of *nomen* for Priscian, the latter says: "adjectives are so called because they are customarily adjoined to other common names which signify substances, or even to proper names, in order to make plain quality or quantity possessed which can increase or decrease without the abolition of the substance" (*KII* 58.20.24, cf. *KII* 84.4.5). This in itself might have afforded temporary satisfaction, had not Priscian unfortunately added "*sapiens grammaticus*" as an example; i.e. "*grammaticus*" is the "common name which signifies a substance" to which "*sapiens*" (a paronymous adjective) has been adjoined (*KII* 58.24). But "*grammaticus*" was one of the logicians' stock examples of a paronym, i.e. it was classed with "white", which, as we have seen, was said by Aristotle to signify a quality and nothing but a quality. How then can it at the same time signify a substance, as Priscian states? In another place Priscian had asserted that the peculiar property of names is that they signify substance and quality (*KII* 55.6), and on one interpretation this is still at variance with the logicians' account of paronyms. In Anselm's time, given the looseness of Boethius' description of paronyms, as well as the latter writer's already-noted concession that "man" signifies certain qualities, an obvious and naive attitude in the face of these incompatibilities would be to ask whether paronyms—especially those which like "*grammaticus*" both qualify and exclusively refer to men—signify substances or qualities.

§4.110 It is with the naive question just suggested, posed in respect of Priscian's unfortunate example ("*grammaticus*") that *De grammatico* opens, and the question itself may rightly be said to arise from confusion in the face of already existing confusion as to the use and status of terms such as "paronym", "signifies", "substance", and "quality", and the sentences in which they occur. Indeed, Anselm wishes that it should appear in this light, since he puts the question into the mouth of a student who can advance and quote opinions to support either alternative, and who goes on, in effect, to pose objections which in themselves point to the source of the confusion. Only a crass disregard of the elucidatory method of the dialogue can have led critics like Maurice to assume that Anselm was unconscious of the ambiguities and incongruities, both explicit and implicit, lurking in that opening question as to whether *grammaticus* is a substance or a quality—a question which becomes even more unintelligible than it is intended to be if, with Maurice, one insists on translating *"grammaticus"* as "a grammarian," and so makes the problem read, "Is a grammarian a substance or a quality?". True, Anselm does not overtly represent the dialogue as one which is concerned with a dispute arising out of differences between the statements of logicians and grammarians, yet the discrepancy about *"grammaticus"* would be familiar to his literal-minded contemporaries who had looked at Priscian and Boethius. In any event, Priscian's doctrine that all names signify substance and quality constitutes one of the positions proffered and rejected in the course of the dialogue (4.22, 4.711); the references made to grammarians suggest that Anselm considered them to be persons who might make unjustified complaints concerning his treatment of the matter in hand (4.20, 4.62). Abelard mentions those who appeal to Priscian's doctrine when discussing the meaning of names in general, and of paronyms in particular (A112-114). In fact Abelard's argument at this point is simply an alternative expression of the same problem as that of *De grammatico*. It is noteworthy also that the twelfth-century glossators on Priscian busied themselves about the same question (*HSP*218-9). Far from being an innovator who imported logical considerations into the study of grammar, as has been claimed (*PBT*234), the twelfth-century grammarian Peter Helias had plenty of precedents for such a mixture; indeed, the truth of the matter is that Peter was engaged in disentangling what some of his predecessors, but not Anselm, had already confused (*HSP*215-6). Anselm is quite clear about the descriptive basis of grammar of the sort found in Priscian: it is to such a basis that his term *"usus loquendi"* refers. And his logical determination of *significatio per se,* which he opposes to *usus loquendi* (4.3), will later have its counterpart in the work of the authors on *grammatica speculativa* the prescriptive grammar which on philosophical-logical grounds dictates rather than describes (*GPMA* Ch. VII, iii).

§4.111 The considerations adduced above by no means exhaust the possible reasons for Anselm's interest in paronyms. Anselm's paronyms, like those said by Ockham to be paronyms in a strict sense, are supposed to "signify accidents". An examination of Boethius' statements on definition appears to reveal that although he sometimes mentioned the definition of accidents, and suggests that they may have "substantial" definitions, he gives very little practical details as to how such definitions were to be arrived at or expressed. It is clear from Ch. VII of Aquinas' *De Ente et Essentia* that the last-named author, armed with the full Aristotelian *corpus*, is able to come to confidently Aristotelian decisions in this matter, thanks to the accessibility of the *Metaphysica*. It seems natural to assume, therefore, that the definition of accidents would be a controversial issue during the intervening interval, or at least since the revival of intelligent logical interest. This assumption is confirmed by the closing remarks of *De grammatico*, as well as by certain remarks made by Abelard (*A596.1.2*). Anselm's dialogue hence represents, among other things, his contribution to this discussion.

§4.2 "Grammaticus" *as a paronym*

§4.21 In view of the subsequent development of western European languages, Priscian and the ancient and medieval logicians could scarcely have chosen a more troublesome example of a paronym than "*grammaticus*". The origins of this choice have already been suggested, and it now remains to attempt, for the first time as far as I am aware, to discover a translation of that word which can be used consistently throughout Anselm's dialogue.

§4.22 Since a *grammaticus* is paronymously named from "*grammatica*", both these Latin words must be examined. The second, namely "*grammatica*", has to be understood as an abstract noun: yet its *prima facie* English translation as "grammar" scarcely seems to provide us with such a noun, as in present-day usage it refers to the set of rules provided by grammarians rather than to the quality, state, action, or passion required by the grammatical definition of an abstract noun. This is because the Latin has that duality of meaning which has now disappeared from "grammar", a duality also possessed by the generic word *"scientia"*, or by *"science"* in Cartesian French. In the same way as these latter were used to refer either to the coherent findings of a given type of research *or* as dispositional words to indicate a person's mental capacities, so also *"grammatica"*, being the name of a particular *"scientia"*, signifies either the rules of grammar *or* that "quality of the soul" which is necessary to operate in accordance with those rules (*B*170A,172A, 169B, 173D, 174B). The second sense has lingered in the French *"grammaire"* until the nineteenth century, since Littré gives what is, in effect, this meaning to the word: for Larousse it is now the art or the book concerned with correct speech and writing. Thus, while "grammar" would serve for the first sense of *"grammatica"*, a word like "literacy", which is the name of a personal quality, is needed in order to reproduce in English the sense for the most part envisaged by Anselm. "Literacy", it will be found, can be used consistently throughout the dialogue as the translation of *"grammatica"*, and this even at those few points where the first sense (i.e. "grammar") is in question. True, it is only in terms of this latter sense that one can be said to know or not to know *grammatica* (4.20, 4.24, 4.31), but if it is desired to remain within a cluster of English words having a strict correlation with the corresponding Latin ones, expressions such as "displaying literacy" seem to be called for at points where knowledge of *grammatica* is in question; e.g. *"homo sciens grammaticam"* (4.240) may be rendered, "man displaying literacy".

§4.221   What now of *"grammaticus"*? In its case the development of language reflects the problem of paronyms: whereas, in Latin, *"grammatica"* has only *"grammaticus"* as its cognate *nomen*, modern French, German and English, for instance, now split the translation of *"grammaticus"* into two alternatives, namely noun and adjective. It is as though the dialogue's question, "Is *grammaticus* a quality or a substance?" had been answered by the provision of adjectival and nominal translations which cater for both alternatives. Thus in English we find, correlated with the word "grammar", both the adjective "grammatical" and the noun "grammarian", either of which could count as the corresponding paronym, with similar alternatives in the other languages mentioned. Under these circumstances, especially when the requisite senses of "is" or "signify" have not been distinguished, and the nominal uses of adjectives are left in the background, the alternative chosen in the translation superficially settles the question, making it utterly trite: if "grammatical" is chosen, then *"grammaticus"* is seen as a quality-word, whereas the choice of "grammarian" makes it appear to be a substance-word. This accident of the history of language accounts for some, but not all, of the horror of those critics of the dialogue who were mentioned in §1.

§4.222   This situation is remedied, and the problem resumes somewhat its original pattern, if *"grammatica"* having been translated as "literacy", *"grammaticus"* now becomes "literate". The latter has a fairly well-established nominal use, and so reproduces the possibility of *"grammaticus"* having reference to human beings when this is envisaged in the corresponding case in the Latin. True, "literate", when used as a noun-translation of *"grammaticus"*, must take on its strong sense, which the French *"lettré"* possesses exclusively, of a "literary man", rather than someone who, in contrast to an illiterate, can merely read. Even in the absence of any objection to the translation of *"grammaticus"* by "grammarian", this still need not necessarily be a more accurate translation than "literate": "scholar", "philologist", or even merely "educated (person)" are alternatives which illustrate its range of meaning. None of these, however, have the ready substantival and adjectival senses possessed by "literate", and which reflect the concern of the dialogue. Boethius' equation of *"grammatica"* and *"grammaticus"* with *"litteratura"* and *"litteratus"* respectively, further encourages the choice of "literacy" and "literate" (*BC*257C-D; cf. Sergius on Donatus, *KIV* 486.15-487.2). Other words which have the ready dual substantival and adjectival senses, and which might have served as translations for *"grammaticus"* were it not for their rather more specialised uses, are "academic", "intellectual", and "scholastic".

§4.223   The peculiar suitability, from a logical point of view, of "literate" as an example in a discussion of meaning, is readily apparent. It so happens as a matter of fact that the only beings of which this paronym is predicated, or to which it is used to refer, are human beings, with the result that one may very well be tempted to hold, like Priscian and the recent traditional logicians when faced with the same kind of situation, that it has "man" (a "substance") as part of its meaning. However, "white" is also a paronym, yet the diversity of white objects to which this word happens to apply is such that there is no corresponding temptation in its case (4.24121). This difference provides Anselm with an excellent pointer to the various meanings of "meaning" which he distinguishes in *De grammatico*: there is the secondary (*per aliud*) sense of "meaning" which involves, where this is possible, generalisation from concrete utterances, *usus loquendi;* this is contrasted with the primary (*per se*) sense of meaning which embodies the requirements of the word's satisfactory functioning in the language (4.23). The latter is the concern of logicians, and he leaves the conclusion to be drawn that the first typifies the activities of grammarians.

§4.3   *Paronyms in recent traditional logic*

§4.311   The term "traditional logic" has for many years been current in order to distinguish the work of the "symbolic" or "mathematical" logicians from that of those who continued in the pre-mathematical discipline. This has resulted in the tendency to lump together all logic of the type current before, say, the work of George Boole (1815-1864) as "traditional", in contradistinction to the new symbolic disciplines. However, some discrimination must be effected within this so-called "traditional" stream, since the concerns of medieval and ancient logicians were often much closer to those arising from certain forms of "mathematical" logic than were those of the "traditional" logicians of the past two or three hundred years. Hence it is to the latter alone that the phrase "traditional logic" is here intended to apply.

§4.312   Exactly the same puzzles about the meaning of paronyms as have been noted in §4.1 are to be discerned in the works of traditional logicians, notwithstanding a certain narrowing of interest under the guise of a different terminology, namely, that of the doctrine of "terms". However, these puzzles already assume an importance more than merely historical when it is recalled that much of contemporary controversy arises directly or indirectly out of problems originally expressed in the vocabulary of the doctrine of terms. Recent traditional logic considers in detail the meanings of words insofar as they function as "subjects" and "predicates" in categorical propositions, i.e. insofar as they can appear in the places of "S" and "P" in the forms "All S is P", "No S is P", "Some S is P", and "Some S is not P". "Terms" are words or groups of words which can thus function, and the classification of terms according to their meanings (in various senses of "meaning") is assumed to be a necessary preliminary to the remaining parts of traditional logic, such as syllogistic. Anselm examines the meanings of words without appearing to have any such preoccupation, thus remaining more close to what was probably the original intention of Aristotle's *Categoriae* before it was rammed into place as a preliminary to the study of two other canonical divisions of traditional logic, namely "Propositions" (or "Judgments") and "Inference" (cf. *KF* Ch.II). Anselm uses syllogistic forms, part of the traditional doctrine of inference, to discuss meaning, but there is no suggestion that the findings of such discussion are seen as a preliminary to syllogistic. On the contrary, not only does his use of the syllogism in such discussion imply his assumption of an already-established syllogistic, and not one which is somehow posterior, but he also makes remarks which, when coupled with his practice, amount to a recognition that standard categorical syllogistic is comparatively elementary (cf. 3.33, 3.6). Further, few of his examples of concrete utterance in any way approach canonical categorical form (e.g. 4.20, 4.421, 4.23). Finally, he is not primarily concerned with the nature of categorical predication, although some of his distinctions do have important reprecussions in that they clarify the status of functors involved in certain sorts of predication.

§4.313   Terms are distinguished as being of the abstract, concrete, and attributive sorts by H.W.B. Joseph, a representative of the traditional school, thus: "terms verbal . . . must be divided into *abstract, concrete,* and *attributive.* A concrete term (verbal) is the name of a person or thing, an abstract term the name of a quality or attribute or relation; so that the distinction between a thing and its qualities, between substance and attribute or relation, is the basis of the distinction between concrete and abstract terms" (*JL*28-29). "Besides abstract and concrete terms verbal, there is a kind of terms verbal which cannot well be classified with either, viz. adjectives and adjectival terms. These are called *attributive* terms, e.g. *red, beaten, insolvent.* They are not the names of qualities like *redness, defeat, insolvency;* on the other hand, it is these qualities which furnish their meaning, not the nature of the various kinds of object to which the qualities may belong. Thus cloth may be red and so may silk, but we would not explain what is meant by calling them red if we were to explain the nature either of silk or cloth; and a man may be insolvent and so may a company, but to explain what is meant by calling them insolvent we must explain the nature not of man, nor of company, but of insolvency" (*JL*36-37). Clearly Joseph's concrete terms are intended to be co-extensive with the substance-signifying words of the ancients, and the attributives at least include, or are co-extensive with, the paronyms—even with paronyms in the narrow sense apparently envisaged by Boethius, to judge by the examples given. Immediately these definitions have been posited, the discussion opens on what is, in effect, the by now age-old topic of the meaning of paronyms: "J. S. Mill held that adjectives are really concrete, on the ground the 'white' is predicated, or is the name, of snow, milk, linen, and not of their colour; that it is an army and not a defeat that is beaten" (*JL*37). Here Joseph is calling attention to Mill's doctrine, already noted, that paronyms and substance-signifying words are of the same sort, and Joseph goes on to attack Mill's view that paronyms signify substances: "In language . . . there are words which, though they can be used as predicates, and therefore satisfy the definition of a term verbal, are not properly names either of a substance or of an attribute. Adjectives are such words" (*JL*37); "The whole question of the separate character of the adjective, or adjectival word, belongs indeed rather to grammar than to logic. But when 'term' means name, or term verbal, as these are either substantival or adjectival, and the concrete and abstract are both substantival, some place is wanted for the the adjectival, and so they are classed separately as attributive terms. If their form were to be ignored, they should rather be considered abstract than (as J.S. Mill would have it) concrete; for their invention implies the consideration of some quality or character in the thing in abstraction from the rest of the thing's nature" (*JL*38). These quotations, and the whole tenor of Joseph's account, show that he is inclined to the view that paronyms signify qualities rather than substances. Yet a certain uneasiness subsists, and this for two reasons. In the first place, this account has been based on the overt selection of blatantly adjectival words—on grammatical adjectives, in fact—with the result that when he encounters words which in a broad sense are paronymous, and are certainly akin to "literate" in that their application is primarily restricted to human beings, viz: "father", "musician" (*JL*37, note 1), "traitor", and "artist" (*JL*155, note 1), a certain hesitation occurs: "terms like *father* or *musician* are adjectival in sense, and would by some be classed as attributive; for though they are substantives, and are predicated of concrete things, they do not primarily signify the concrete things of which they are predicated; a father must be somewhat else, to be a father" (*JL*37, note 1; cf. *JL*20 note 2). Secondly, as the quotations given above show all too clearly, the grammatically nominal uses of adjectives are overlooked, so that the possibility of some kind of kinship between attributive terms and cases like the substantives just-mentioned is generally missed. But it is precisely when the grammatically substantive, broadly paronymous, "father" and "musician", rather than purely adjectival paronyms are in question, that he comes much closer to an appreciation applicable to paronyms in general. It is in a belated footnote that he goes further and finally recognises the grammatically nominal functions of adjectives, and even here, significantly enough, gives a Latin example, but without making explicit the possibility of inflection as a device for forming nouns from adjectives in English: "Adjectives can indeed be used as subjects, e.g. *Beati immaculati in via,* where it is possible to take either term as predicate. In many languages an article is generally necessary in order to make an adjective do duty as substantive" (*JL*38, note 2). In general, therefore, Joseph tends to assimilate attributive terms to grammatical adjectives, and leaves in the background the possible grammatically nominal function of such adjectives ("they [i.e. attributive terms] can be used as predicates, and . . . are not properly names either of a substance or an attribute" (*JL*37). As a result, when other loosely paronymous words, this time grammatically substantive, are in question, he is not altogether committed to classifying them as attributive. A grammatical distinction which could itself be bridged by those other grammatical rules which he tends to neglect (prefixing of article to, nominal inflection of, adjectives) hence causes him to separate adjectives and substantives, thereby blinding him to the possibility of that logical community of at least some substantives with adjectives, which Anselm's theory of the signification of paronyms suggests; (compare, for example, Anselm's thesis as to the parity of *"albus"* and *"grammaticus"* (3.94, 4.24121)). Cook Wilson, in his often acute criticism of the doctrine of terms, appears to suffer from the same sort of bias. He is very emphatic that adjectival paronyms neither name anything nor, in the traditional terminololgy, "denote" anything (*WJC*390, 397, 402); but the grammarian could at least draw the attention of this classicist and man and military interests to the use of "heavies" to refer to large-bore, long-range, pieces of ordnance. The veil of "improper use" or appeal to the grammatical distinction between "heavy" and "heavies" (adjective and noun) is of no logical service, since as Joseph has in effect reminded us above, the nominal use of the translations of both would be perfectly proper in Latin, for instance. True, at one point he does mention "The noun 'blue'", but only as an equivalent of "blueness" (*WJC*402); this equivalence, while displaying an interesting *prima facie* community with Anselm's scandalous *"grammaticus est grammatica"* (cf. §5.3) is nevertheless not linked with anything like Anselm's appreciation of the nominal function of paronyms.

§4.314 In contrast, grammatical categories appear to have influenced J.S. Mill in a direction opposed to that of Joseph on the topic of attributive terms (and hence of paronyms). While Joseph tended to stress the opposition between substantive and adjective, name and predicate, Mill starts with the supposition that terms must invariably be names, and hence name something: " . . . the first glance at a proposition shows that it is formed by putting together two names". After this incautious admission, with its glaringly false result, he continues, "The predicate is the name denoting that which is affirmed or denied. The subject is the name denoting the person or thing which something is affirmed or denied of" (*MSLI*, Ch.1, §2). This name-doctrine is applied to uninflected adjectives and adjectives unpreceded by an article, with the result that they have to be translated in order to perform the denoting: ". . . there is no difference of meaning between *round* and *a round object*, it is only custom which prescribes that on any given occasion one shall be used, and not the other. We shall therefore, without scruple, speak of adjectives as names . . ." (*MSLI*, Ch.II, §2). Hence for Mill all terms, including attributives, name something: attributives and substantives, paronyms and other concrete names, are all of the same sort. At the same time he recognises the kind of contention later advanced by Joseph, i.e. that qualities are somehow involved in the meaning of adjectives, as well as the Aristotelian-Boethian point that even substantives somehow signify qualities, and this, combined with his name-theory of terms, results in the doctrine of connotation and denotation: "A non-connotative term is one which signifies a subject only, or an attribute only. A connotative term is one which denotes a subject, and implies an attribute. By a subject is meant anything which possesses attributes. Thus 'John' or 'London', or 'England', are names which signify a subject only. 'Whiteness',

'Length', 'Virtue', signify an attribute only. None of these names, therefore are connotative. But 'white', 'long', 'virtuous' are connotative. The word 'white' denotes all white things, as snow, paper, the foam of the sea, &c., and implies, or as it was termed by the schoolmen *connotes*, the attribute *whiteness*. The word 'white' is not predicated of the attribute, but of the subjects, snow, &c.; but when we predicate it of them, we imply, or connote, that the attribute whiteness belongs to them . . . All concrete general names are connotative. The word 'man', for example, denotes Peter, James, John, and an indefinite number of other individuals of whom, taken as a class, it is the name. But it is applied to them, because they possess, and to signify that they possess, certain attributes. These seem to be, corporeity, animal life, rationality, and a certain external form, which for distinction we call the human . . . The word 'man', therefore, signifies all these attributes, and all subjects which possess these attributes" (*MSLI* Ch. II, §5). This amounts to a resolution of the question "Do paronyms signify substances or qualities?", which like Priscian's general doctrine of names (KII55.6) admits the claims of both alternatives; all terms, including paronyms, but excluding abstract and proper names, are such that subjects (substances) are denoted and qualities connoted: "The name 'man' therefore, is said to signify the subjects directly, the attributes indirectly; it denotes the subjects, and implies, or involves, or indicates, or as we shall say henceforth, *connotes*, the attributes. It is a connotative name. Connotative names have hence also been called *denominative* [i.e. paronymous], because the subject which they denote is denominated by, or receives a name from, the attribute which they connote" (*MSLI*, Ch. II, §5). In fact, as Mill's use of "denominative" here shows, his equation of connotative names and denominative names (i.e. paronyms) leads to the elimination of any possibility of that distinction between sorts of common names which Anselm was at pains to stress by means of the notion of paronymy.

§4.3141   In short, although the term "paronym" may be altogether satisfactory as a classificatory heading for logical purposes, it at least permits the possibility of a community between grammatical adjectives and certain concrete nouns—a possibility which Joseph misses because of his insistence on the grammatical distinction between adjective and name. At the same time the notion of paronymy is capable of effecting exactly that division within the logician's non-abstract "names" (which include grammatical adjectives) the possibility of which Mill's insistence on the nominal nature of all "connotative" terms caused him to overlook. Were it not for the fact the Mill's and Priscian's theories of the signification of names overlap to some extent, the way in which *De grammatico* states (4.22) what is in effect Mill's position and some of its consequences before attacking them might appear to be a remarkable anticipation. Likewise, the insistence on the part of Mill that in order to become names, adjectives should have added to them the names of what they name, as when "round" becomes "round object" is redolent of the Student's contention that "literate" means "literate man" (4.240). Keynes shares this position, or is at least appealing to its pre-theoretical basis, when he makes the suggestion "that in such propositions as 'the rich are not be envied', 'the rich' is equivalent to 'rich persons'" (*KSE*8). This insistence that meanings are to be regulated by generalisation from reference alone constitutes an arbitrary restriction on the flexibility of the language (cf. §5.410).

§4.32   Such are the terms in which the narrower aspect of the dispute of *De grammatico* has in more recent times been revived anew. Mill proclaims the medieval origin of his vocabulary (*MSL* 42-43), and it is clear that the dispute remained alive throughout the middle ages (*MID*46, note 1, *JL*156-8). It is in this perennial background of obscurity that contemporary discussions, in many ways a continuation of the old, have their origin, with the vocabulary of synonymy, meaning, sense, and reference gradually replacing that of connotation and denotation. Anselm's dialogue, the most despised of his works, states the problem in all its aspects, broad and narrow, and although avowedly no more than tentative sparring (4.83), minutely explores the possibilities and proposes answers still relevant to the present state of the discussion; indeed, had those answers been properly understood and developed, much of the obscurity of the intervening centuries might have been avoided.

V

THE DOCTRINE OF *DE GRAMMATICO:*
INFORMAL EXPOSITION

§5.01   An analysis of the doctrine of *De grammatico* in terms of a modern logical language is presented in §6. However, for the purpose of providing an easily assimilable account of that doctrine, the present section attempts an exposition of its central thesis in a simple, informal, manner, underpinned by cross-reference to the matter of previous sections as well as to the ampler details given in §6; the defects of informal exposition will thus be compensated for by the unitary presentation of much material the interrelationship of which might not otherwise have been immediately apparent. At the same time the explanations here given may be of use to those who have no inclination to follow through in detail the logical co-ordinates provided in §6.

§5.10   I am informed by my current University Diary that Congo the Chimp has been elected Honorary President of the University's Psychological Society. As far as I know, this is a new use of the word "president", and might give rise to reflection. Is the meaning of that word affected by this new use, and if so, in what way? Again, suppose the craze for non-human presidents spread, with the result that the philosophers made the Owl of Minerva Honorary

President of their society: would the election of this non-existent
animal also affect the meaning of "president"? Of course, it all depends on what you mean by "meaning", and on what kind of discussions you conceive discussions which terminate in a decision on
meaning to be. In attempting to sketch the characteristic features
of the central doctrine of *De grammatico* I shall in fact be outlining
Anselm's position in the face of problems such as these: in order
to fill in the background I have had to draw upon the works of
other writers of the period, although the specifically Anselmian
contribution to the discussion has a value and interest which can
be considered quite apart from its dependence on such a background.

§5.11   Saint Anselm, in common with other medieval logicians,
appears to have felt that discussion of meaning involved the taking
into consideration of two *prima facie* incompatible ideals: accounts
of meaning should reflect how things are and yet at the same time
should not have to be constantly revised to accord with changes in
states of affairs, as when a chimpanzee becomes a president. The
second of these ideals is, as we shall see, one of the mainsprings of
the dialogue.

§5.2   The way in which Anselm and the other medievals attempted to reconcile the two ideals mentioned may be approached
by way of their notion that common names (including the grammarian's adjectives) can be roughly divided into two classes, namely
those which express a certain sort of incompleteness, and those
which do not. Here I am translating Anselm's words *indigentia*—
needfulness—as "incompleteness" (4.230). The sense of "incompleteness" intended can be illustrated by means of Anselm's own
examples and by reference to the commentary on the *Posterior
Analytics* given by Aquinas, who elsewhere uses the Latin word
"incompleta" in respect of the *definitio* which such a case calls
for (4.42; cf. *APA*87,259,281,289,295 and *ADEE* Cap. VII).
Thus, if I were to announce to someone that there were some
whites shut up in a certain building, then my hearer would be
making a perfectly sensible move if he were to ask what the whites

were which were thus enclosed (4.421). Of course, in given contexts, e.g. in South Africa at present, or in the wash-house on the
morning of a washing-day, talk about whites would immediately
call forth the assumption on the part of the hearer that white *men*
or white *clothes* were being talked about; Anselm deals with this
kind of contextual, habitual association quite competently (cf.
§5.42), but it is taken to be not available for the purposes of this
example. In Aquinas' terms, in such a situation one can sensibly
ask, "What is the something else (*alterum aliquid*) which is white?"
(APA281). This possibility is a symptom of the incompleteness now
in question, an incompleteness which is also treated at great length
by Boethius and Aristotle. So far the colour-word "white" has been
used as an example, since it has as feasible a ring in English, with
its ready nominal use in the plural (cf.§4.107), as have Latin adjectives, whether singular or plural, practically any one of which,
when the subject of an assertion, leaves open the same question.
Words expressing shape (e.g. "oval") or state (e.g. "hot"), although
not so readily used as sentence-subjects in English, are other examples of words which carry with them the same openness, the
same incompleteness; indeed, if "oval" or "hot" were given as answers to a "What is the something else . . . ?" question, the ques-
tioner could still carry on with further such questions. Their possibility only comes to an end (in pre-theoretical discourse) when
names of a contrasting sort, namely those which express completeness, are given in the reply. Names of this sort, because of the manner in which the distinction is now being introduced, may be called
"stop-names", or may be said to name completive objects, in that
they do not leave open the possibility of further "What is the something else . . . ?" questions. Examples of such stop-names proffered
by Anselm are "man", "horse", and "stone", the first two of which are
also used by a modern author who makes precisely the same point:
". . . whatever is correctly called, e.g. a man or a horse, is just a man
or a horse, not something else to which properties are ascribed"
(MP300-301). Other means of distinguishing between the two classes of names are also sometimes helpful: for instance, ostensive indication is more straightforward in the case of things named by stop-

names than in the case of things not so named (4.14, cf. W35). Again, in respect of the former one can sensibly ask the question "How many?", but not in respect of the latter, (*ASTI*, q.39, art. 3, cf. *AG3P*86). Aquinas also adds that things *become* white, for instance, in that there was a time at which something now white was not white, whereas there was no time at which something now a man was not a man (using "man" in the sense of "human being"). If, corresponding to this division in sorts of names, one also recognises a distinction between the sorts of theories centred round those names, one means of partly reconciling the two ideals of the last paragraph can be glimpsed. The theories which relate to completive objects can be relied upon to preserve stability, in particular as regards the definitions which form part of those theories. Revision in accordance with changes in states of affairs need not be anticipated in such cases, to which the classical system of definition by means of *genus*, *species*, and *differentia*, was applicable; the definitional frameworks here presupposed appear to have taken the form of strong identities (defined §6.22.10) or some one or other of their inferential equivalents, i.e. the existence of something named by the *definiens* was required for their truth. This separation is a partial solution to the problem, but there still remains the question how the definitions of things which are not completive objects, and which perhaps do not even exist, are to be formulated in such a manner that revision need not follow upon new uses, new applications. Anselm's discussion in *De grammatico* centres round just this difficulty, which had not been fully resolved in the logical writings of Aristotle, and the commentaries thereon, as bequeathed to the Latin West by Boethius. The further suggestions of Aristotle, which are contained in his *Metaphysica*, were not available until the recovery of the full *corpus* of his works. It is of these that Aquinas makes use when dealing with the same difficulty in Ch.VII of his *De Ente et Essentia*.

§5.301   The characteristic Anselmian statement of the problem of the definitions of things other than completive objects is framed in terms of the ancient usage, described in detail in §4.1, which authorises "paronym" (*nomen denominativum*) as a term applicable to those names imposed on account of the possession of the quality named by the abstract noun corresponding to the name, as when a man is called "brave" because of his bravery: English adjectives are therefore paronyms, as also are those concrete nouns (most of which apply exclusively to human beings) having a corresponding abstract noun, e.g. "hero" and "rascal". If names imposed on account of something's being in a certain state are also allowed, for similar reasons, to count as paronyms, then examples like "bachelor", "spinster", and "president" come within the scope of the notion of paronymy. It has to be assumed that the manufacture of abstract nouns by the addition of suffixes such as "-hood", "-ness", "-ity", or "*-eitas*" to those concrete nouns not already having such a corresponding abstract noun is barred. Hence it is plain that the development of natural language for philosophical purposes has made the distinction between paronyms and other shared names highly contingent: thus, if we are to follow Anselm's point we must postulate that "man" is not paronymous, in spite of the high medieval assumption, shared by J.S. Mill, but not by Locke, that the presence in the language of "humanity" ("*humanitas*") made it so—an assumption not prevalent in the eleventh century (*ASTI*, q.37, art.2, c.; *MSLI* Ch.2, §5, *LEIII* Ch. 8, §2). From another point of view the distinction is not so contingent. In the common course of utterance one may well have occasion to compare the qualities of one object with those of another (cf.3.111,3.112), or to speak of the beginning, duration, or termination of a state, but no such occasions occur for the use of the philosopher's artificial abstract nouns, such as "dogness", "stoneness", "*lapideitas*", and so forth (§4.108). Paronyms roughly correspond, then, to the nineteenth century logicians' "attributive" terms, and other shared names to their "concrete" terms, and to my "stop-names" (§4.3). The opening question of *De grammatico*, namely, "Whether *grammaticus* is substance or quality" is in effect a question posed concerning a specimen paronym ("*grammaticus*") which appears to invalidate this correspondence, since the decision that *grammaticus* is substance would mean that "*grammaticus*", unlike most of its fellow-paronyms, had turned out to be a stop-name, and hence required a sort of theory with definitions like those associated with other stop-names such as

"man". The equation (just implied) of substance-names with what
have hitherto been called "stop-names" has been held off for as long
as possible in order to avoid the misleading impressions which might
arise from Locke's having infected the term "substance" with a sense
clean contrary to that which it has in medieval writings. Locke gets
his "unknown somewhat" story of substance precisely because he
insists, like his own "Indian philosopher", on pressing forward with
the "What is the something else . . . ?" questions exactly at the points
where those questions become inappropriate, i.e. by treating what
I have called "stop-words" as though they were signals to carry
on (*LEII*, Ch.23, §3). Only empty variable-words like "thing" and
"it" finally remain to function in the answers. With a procedure
so devised it becomes the most unsurprising of truisms that "substance" must hence be an "unknown somewhat"; it could not be
otherwise.

§5.3011   Notwithstanding its obsolescence and contingency, the division between paronyms and other shared names serves to circum-
scribe a class of terms which have been the topic of dispute for the
last one and a half thousand years, and which still appear in current discussions on synonymy. In antiquity the dispute was between
logicians and grammarians: for the former, paronyms "signify a
quality", but according to Priscian paronyms, like all names, signify
substance and quality, and he was prepared to treat a paronym
which applies exclusively to human beings, namely the very "*grammaticus*" which is the concern of *De grammatico*, as a name which
signifies a substance (*KII* 58.24, cf. §4.108). Abelard notes this discrepancy (*AII*3.19.24, cf. §4.109), the discussion of which centred,
in recent "traditional" logic, on the function of attributive terms
(cf. §4.3).

§5.31   Within the framework described, Anselm provides an interpretation of the dialogue's opening question which not only solves
the definitional difficulties which have been described, but also illuminates his view of the peculiar nature of his discussion—a view
which is in evidence as from the very first words of the dialogue:

"grammaticus is substance" and *"grammaticus* is quality" are the two alternative verdicts which its opening question brings into play. The first of these one might at a pinch let pass as sensible, temporarily shelving any qualms about "substance", but the second is plain nonsense, as may be seen more clearly if one asks, "Which is the quality that *grammaticus* is?"; the reply can only be *"grammatica"*, so that one is left, in Latin, with *"grammaticus est grammatica"* which is grammatically so awry that the possibility of its being true seems to be altogether out of the question (4.5022, 4.2341). Yet Anselm's thesis in fact is that nonsense of this sort may intervene in the resolution of the problem of paronymous definition, given the conditions outlined—a thesis of the sort which John of Salisbury argues against in his *Metalogicon.* The very queerness of the locutions which have just been mentioned is sufficient to shock one into the realisation that the sentence which was allowed to pass, namely, *"grammaticus* is substance", likewise exemplifies a similar queerness beneath the veil of its grammatical congruity. Anselm's deliberate advocacy of nonsense for logical purposes, an advocacy which will be shown to have a sound enough basis, is the source of the confusion and amazement on the part of past critics of the dialogue who have been at a loss, from the outset, as to how to produce a sensible translation of that nonsense. Such a sensible translation could only be a mistranslation, since apart from the comparatively ordinary trouble about the translation of *"grammaticus"* into English and other modern European languages (§4.2), the peculiarly logical sentences in which it occurs (*"grammaticus* is quality", *"grammaticus est grammatica"*) are, according to Anselm himself, of forms which do not accord with ordinary usage (*usus loquendi*) (4.2341). Hence, so as to reproduce more accurately the effect of the original Latin, and at the same time to avoid the selection of what might turn out to be a misleading piece of English nonsense, the present account for the most part leaves the shared name *"grammaticus"* and the abstract noun *"grammatica"* untranslated, and gives only minimal translations, unadorned by logically loaded articles or possessive adjectives, of sentences in which they occur.

§5.320   Not only does Anselm consider that nonsense is called for in his dialectical theorising; he claims to find it actually existing in, or entailed by, the writings of his predecessors, Aristotle and Boethius (4.5122; cf.4.515, 4.600). Such writers, complains the Student of the dialogue, propound in their books things which they would blush to assert in ordinary conversation (4.210); they often make the assertion that *grammaticus* is quality, or the inferentially equivalent assertion "'*grammaticus*' signifies quality" (4.60), when the usage of common speech shows that "*grammaticus* is substance" (i.e. man)—whence also "'*grammaticus*' signifies substance"—is a more appropriate verdict (4.212). After all, if "*grammaticus est grammatica*" and "'*grammaticus*' signifies *grammatica*" are true, then we ought to be able to replace "*grammaticus*" by "*grammatica*" in true sentences, and so use "*grammaticus*" to refer to *grammatica;* yet this plainly produces nonsense such as "That man is good at *grammaticus*", and "*Grammaticus* is a useful sort of knowledge"— assertions which if made in the company of ordinary folk would annoy the *grammatici* and even draw guffaws from peasants (4.20). In reply to such complaints, the disastrous consequences of which for ordinary speech he would deny (4.620, 4.621), the Tutor of the dialogue applies to the case of names the quite general distinction which for Anselm also extends to verbs (predicates), namely the distinction between signification properly so called, precisive (*per se*) signification, and signification in an oblique, improper (*per aliud*) sense of the word (4.232). In the case of paronyms, the oblique signification of the name is its reference (4.233); this is given in and determined by the current course of utterance, and is a reference made to objects (4.2341). Precisive signification, in the determination of which nonsense becomes appropriate, or which appears to have nonsense as its consequence, is hence sharply distinguished from reference (*appellatio*); thus "*grammaticus*" does not refer to *grammatica,* even though "*grammaticus est grammatica*" and "'*grammaticus*' signifies (precisively) *grammatica*" are both true (4.2340). Precisive signification is stated in the metalinguistic correlates of assertions such as "*grammaticus est grammatica*", which are intratheoretical in respect of the names in question (4.430, 4.515), whereas reference is extra-theoretical in respect of names (4.24121,4.430, 4.515). Thus the fact that *"grammaticus"* happens to apply exclusively to human beings is not part of the theory of *grammaticus;* this claim as to the extra-theoretical nature of the reference of paronyms will be the clue to the satisfaction of their definitional requirements.

§5.321　The manner in which Anselm defends his thesis that nonsense can have a place in logical discussion affords a means of grasping more clearly the nature of the distinctions so far outlined. Thus, guided by *usus loquendi,* by the way in which *"grammaticus"* is in fact used in ordinary non-technical speech, the Student claims that *grammaticus* should be defined as *homo sciens grammaticam;* after all, no one ever uses *"grammaticus"* to refer to an illiterate man or to literacy apart from the men who have it (4.420). This argument is opposed by the Tutor in various ways: it bars the possibility of new applications of *"grammaticus"* (4.2412), gives rise to infinite regress (4.2414), and cannot be generalised in respect of all paronyms (4.2415). The most important argument, however, turns on whether *"grammaticus"* can be said to name a species of human being in the strict Boethian sense of "species" (4.2411). The details of this discussion need not concern us here; its importance lies in the fact that it reminds us of the technical apparatus of *genera, species,* and *differentiae,* which lies behind the theory of definition in terms of which the discussion is proceeding at this point. It can be shown, by reference to an artificial language sufficiently rich in definable parts of speech (semantical categories), that discourse at a pre-definitional stage of the sort here in question does in fact necessitate recourse to parts of speech which either do not occur in the current course of utterance, or which, if they do occur, are not distinguished by ordinary grammar. An artificial language which meets these requirements is the Ontology of S. Le'sniewski in terms of which C. Lejewski has shown the precise way in which the "is" of *"man* is (a) species", for instance, is a functor of a semantical category quite diverse from that of the "is" of a sentence such as "Socrates is (a) philosopher" (*LA*247-249); both are proposition-forming functors, but the first, the higher-order "is", has functors (predicates, verbs) as arguments, while the second, of lower order, has names (cf.§6.22.15). Boethius, in the course of his commentaries, not only uses the "is" of higher semantical category, but also displays some realisation of its novelty at at least three points, although he is of course at a loss to determine precisely the nature of this novelty (*B*201A-202A, *B*176D, *B*309C-310B; cf. §6.22); in Ontology the first, the unusual "is", is definable ultimately in terms of the second, the more usual "is" (*LA*249, §6.22.15). It is therefore not at all beyond the bounds of possibility that Anselm who, like Boethius, of course uses the higher "is", also grasps the difference, and with only a natural language at his disposal displays the originality of genius by resorting to the shock of the violation of current forms of utterance in order to show that semantical categories of a type quite diverse from those recognised by the grammar of current speech are required in order to deal satisfactorily with the definitional problems which confront him.

§5.322   The possibility just mooted becomes an unavoidable conclusion when the material of the remainder of the dialogue, and the order in which it is presented, are considered. Thus the Tutor, having shown by means of the arguments briefly referred to in the last paragraph, that *"homo"* must be eliminated from the Student's suggested *homo sciens grammaticam* definition of *grammaticus* accordingly truncates that definition to read " . . . *sciens grammaticam"*, and states that because *"grammaticus"* signifies *sciens grammaticam*, it therefore signifies *grammatica* (4.31). At first sight this would seem to be an exceedingly slippery way of supporting the thesis that *grammaticus est grammatica,* since the latter has now been arrived at by way of a statement about signification having *"grammaticus est sciens grammaticam"* as its *de re* correlate (cf.4.601-4.603), and both of the latter appear to be in perfect accord with ordinary usage; indeed, the sentence *"omne sciens grammaticam est grammaticum"* has quite properly been allowed to pass at an earlier point in the discussion without any objection on this score (4.24120). However, *De Veritate* 12 shows that Anselm was well-versed in the grammar of participles and participial forms such as the one now in question, and so would be familiar with Priscian's doctrine that participles are by nature a cross between verbs (i.e. what would logically be classified as functors) and names; they are called participles because they participate in the nature of both verb and noun (KII 551.4.10). This suggests that Anselm is at this point trading on the dual function of participles: *"sciens grammaticam"* is not to be understood here in the plainly nominal sense which it has in a sentence such as *"omne sciens grammaticam est grammaticum"*, but as a verbal, predicative, or functorial form: if this is so, then he is justified in keeping to the fore of the subsequent discussion (as he in fact does) the scandalous *"grammaticus est grammatica"* instead of the innocuous *"grammaticus est sciens grammaticam"*. Both are true, but the *"est"* of the second is susceptible of interpretation in such a way that *"sciens grammaticam"* would be a nominal, and not, as here required, verbal argument of *"est"*, whereas the *"est"* of the first is shown, by the presence of *"grammatica"*, to be of more unusual semantical category. All this would still be little more than conjecture, were it not for the fact that Anselm devotes one of the later sections of the dialogue (4.8) to the demonstration of exactly this point: *"habens albedinem"*, insofar as it is the definition of *"albus"* is not to be interpreted as *"aliquid habens albedinem"* or *"qui habet albedinem,"* i.e. is not to be given the nominal, referring force which it could have in other contexts (4.811). In the course of this demonstration he mentions a case involving terms of the same forms as those of *"omne sciens grammaticam est grammaticum"*, but expanded in two ways in order to bring out the nominal nature of its arguments, namely: *"omnis qui est albus est aliquid habens [albedinem]"*, and *"omnis qui est albus est qui habet [albedinem]"*; this particular truth, he declares, with its nominal arguments, is not in question: the question concerns the definition of *albus*, not extra-theoretical facts about white objects (4.810). This clearly leaves open only the verbal, functorial, facet of the participial forms to function in the definition of things named paronymously: Anselm has gone as far as he can, with only a natural language and ordinary grammar at his disposal, to bring out the nature of the semantical category of the *"est"* of such statements as *"grammaticus est grammatica"*, *"grammaticus est sciens grammaticam"* (in this context), and *"grammaticus est qualitas"*, all of which he would accept as the *de re* equivalents of the *de voce* statements, *" 'grammaticus' est significativum grammaticae"*, *" 'grammaticus' significat scientem grammaticam"*, and *" 'grammaticus' est vox significans qualitatem"* respectively (4.601-4.603, 4.31, 4.-5022). These decisions not only solve the problem of the definition of things named paronymously, as will be shown in §5.410, but also throw light on Anselm's understanding of statements which assert that such-and-such is a quality, or that such-and-such is a substance; it is at least evident that for him such statements are more complex than the simple two-name sentences which their grammatical form might make them appear to be. Most significantly, the Tutor adds that in such contexts one has a *showing* (*ostentatio*) rather than a naming (*nominatio*) of that which is signified by the name in question (4.604). Definitions of functors and arguments having the diverse semantical categories attributable to *"est"* and its arguments, and which Anselm has thus painfully distinguished, are available in Ontology (§6.22).

§5.323   Lest there should be any lingering doubts as to Anselm's full awareness that he is here dealing with what would nowadays also be called "type distinctions", mention has still to be made of the passage in which he employs what is, in effect, the same example as one which Wittgenstein uses in order to illuminate such distinctions (W22). Meaning and use, says the Tutor, are opposed in the sense that logical discourse from which emerge conclusions about the meaning of a name is of a nature diverse from ordinary discourse in which that same name is used to refer to objects (4.620). The kind of diversity he has in mind has already been outlined above, and he continues to drive home his point by reminding the Student that this diversity is no more extraordinary than that which is encountered when grammarians discuss exemplary significant utterances in a fashion which has no repercussions in any account of the structure of things as they are. Thus they assert that *"lapis"* is masculine in gender, *"petra"* feminine, and *"mancipium"* neuter, and that *"timere"* is active in voice, but *"timeri"* passive; yet no one is thereby

tempted to assert that a stone is a masculine object, a rock a fem--
inine one, and possession something neither masculine nor feminine,
or that fearing is an action, and that being feared is the undergoing
of an action (4.620 - 4.621). This passage, referring as it does to
grammatical practice, fits neatly into place in the development of
the dialogue's argument insofar as it is a rejoinder to the Student's
claim, quoted above, that the logicians' assertions would have grammatically catastrophic consequences if taken seriously in the common course of utterance (4.20,§5.320).

§5.401   There still remain many extraordinary riches in the dialogue which, because of their intricacy, and since they do not directly affect the central doctrine, cannot be treated in detail in an
informal exposition. In particular there is the brilliant series of analyses in the course of which Anselm resolves the paradox:

No *grammaticus* can be understood (to be) without *grammatica*

Every man can be understood (to be) without *grammatica*

Hence: No *grammaticus* is a man (3.101 - 3.113)

The resolution involves drawing upon the doctrine that has been
recapitulated above, and while dealing with the complicated expressions which ensue, the Tutor expresses Anselm's recognition
that inferential forms which overflow the bounds of the standard
categorical syllogism can be encountered in inferences which on
the face of things appear to be categorical syllogisms (3.33). This
recognition is all of a piece with the thesis described above to the
effect that parts of speech other than those usually recognised by
ordinary grammar are necessary for the accomplishment of logical
purposes. However, leaving aside such important but relatively
subsidiary features, certain corollaries, some of which occur in Anselm's own text, may now be drawn from the informal exposition
of the central doctrine which has been presented.

§5.410   In the first place it is clear that Anselm's decision that the
definition of things named paronymously should be pitched at the
level of the higher order "is" would allow the fulfilment of the re-

quirement that existence of *definienda* need not be presupposed as a truth-condition of those definitions, and that his adoption of truncated participial forms as arguments of that "is" permits the realisation of the ideal that such definitions should not have to be amended as each new application of the paronyms in question. Thanks to the truncation of the Student's proposed definition of *grammaticus* from *homo sciens grammaticam* to *sciens grammaticam* (4.240, 4.31), the application of "*grammaticus*" to beings other than men is no longer theoretically barred as it would be were the Student's definition to be accepted. At the same time, the semantical category of the "is" mentioned, with its functorial arguments, is not such as to necessitate existential consequences, given the arguments which it must take if the "is"-sentences in which it occurs are to serve as definitions (§5.22.14). This is in contrast to what holds in the case of the more familiar lower-order "is". To put the matter in a slightly more technical fashion: the sentence "for some *a*, *a* is *a*" is a thesis of Ontology, and does not entail the existence of anything when the "is" is of the higher order, and "*a*" is a variable for appropriate arguments; if, however, the "is" is of the lower order (as in "Elizabeth is queen") then the former sentence is not a thesis of Ontology; for "*a* is *a*" then to be true *a* must exist. Since the higher-order "is" is definable ultimately in terms of that of lower order, definitions exploiting the former are still mediately earth-bound, and so continue, in their *de re* way, to reflect how things are, as required in §5.11. "*Grammaticus est grammatica*", scandalous though it may appear from the point of view of *usus loquendi,* secures the consequences mentioned. Its alternative statement ("*grammaticus est sciens grammaticam*"), involving as it does the truncation of "*homo sciens grammaticam*" also constitutes a rational reconstruction of the "What is the something else . . . ?" situation in such a way as to bring out the predicative status of paronyms. Anselm's example of the enclosed white has already been quoted in this connection (§5.2), and has as its counterpart his other example of the white horse and the black bull (4.422, 4.423); thus, if faced with a white horse and a black bull, I were told to strike the white, I would be able to fill the gap in my understanding of "white" (" . . . *habens albedinem"*). I would be able to answer for myself the "What is the something else . . . ?" question by resort to information obtained through the particular sense-experience available in the siuation described; the object, namely the horse, which is in this context referred to by the word "white", can only on that account be said to be "signified" by the word "white" in an improper, oblique, sense (4.4233, 4.4234). From the point of view of precisive signification both "white" and "literate" stand on the same level as regards their referents: the one no more signifies man, horse, or any other species of (completive) object than the other. It just so happens that the only literate beings with which we are acquainted, and to refer to which we use in common speech the name "literate", are human beings; equally contingent is the fact that beings other than men happen to be white. From a purely theoretical standpoint it could just as well be the other way round (4.24121). This aspect of Anselm's distinction between meaning and use (which in the case of names is reference, *appellatio*) somewhat approaches A.M. Mac-Iver's distinction between that which is *symbolised* by words insofar as they are "types", and that which is *suggested* by tokens of those types in particular contexts (*MD*). The difficulty raised by the election of Congo the Chimp vanishes, since if Anselm's example is followed, then *being president* will be defined as *holding presidential office*—a form of definition which leaves open the nature of the species of being to which the word "president" may apply, so that new theories are not made essential by such novel applications. Neither are they made necessary by the election of the Owl of Minerva to the presidency of the philosophers' group; also the higher order "is" associated with the definition need not be an existential "is".

§5.411 In terms of the distinction between intrinsic and extrinsic paronymy (cf. §4.106), the suggestions of the last paragraph apply only to cases of intrinsic paronymy. The new applications of paronyms which may occur in cases of extrinsic paronymy would, as is evident from the examples used by Aquinas, require the incorporation of participles such as *"conservans"*, *"significans"*, and so forth, in their definitions (e.g. *ASTIII* q.60, art.1, c; cf. §4.106). From Anselm's own list of non-strict or "improper" uses of verbs and names one can draw *"valens"*, *"figurans"*, and several other participles which could be incorporated in this way (*SNUW*34.29.39). However, since such uses are said to be "improper", it is evident from the occurence of the same description (*"non proprie"*) in *De grammatico* (4.233), that they would belong to the sphere of *significatio per aliud*, oblique signification, rather than to that of the *significatio per se*, precisive signification, which it is the aim of *De grammatico* to disengage; in fact many of the cases envisaged by Anselm in his list amount to little more than metaphor. On the basis of Anselm's thesis that *"facere"* is to verbs as pronouns are to names (*SNUW*25-28), it is evident that the participle *"faciens"* could serve in a generalisation of paronymous definition, whether instrinsic or extrinsic, proper or metaphorical.

§5.42   The sharp theoretical distinction between meaning (*significatio per se*) and reference (*appellatio*) in respect of paronyms may appear to be excessively severe; it extends even to the point of excluding mention of body or surface from colour definitions. For Anselm, therefore, "Everything green is extended" would not be "analytic" (*Q*32). However, he tempers this severity by a device of a rather Humean sort in order to do justice to the fact that things are as they happen to be, e.g. that only men are literate, that only extended things are coloured, and so on: he claims that an anticipatory or associational disposition is set up in the hearer because of the customary experiential conjunction of the accident signified by the paronym, and its usual bearer (4.4211). In cases of short-term or variable conjunction, like that of the unenclosed white horse, the connection is effected by means of some particular sense-experience (4.423, 4.4234). Aquinas appears (in Ch. VII of his *De Ente et Essentia*) to be prepared to attribute more intelligibility to conjunctions of the sort which Anselm, to judge by *De grammatico*, would treat as blankly associational. The connection thus described by Anselm affects the dichotomy made at the outset between shared names which raise the "What is the something else . . . ?" question, and those which do not (§5.2). This division remains underpinned in theory, but in practice the question will not be asked in the many cases where the context, as represented either by the general structure of things as they happen to be (e.g. only men are literate) or by local spatio-temporal features such as those associated with the use of "whites" in South Africa or in the laundry on washing-day, has been sufficient to set up such a connection. When a language such as English is being used—a language in which adjectives either cannot be used with the same nominal facility as can, say, adjectives in Latin or, if they are so used, soon assume a specialised referential function in respect of one type of object, as in the cases of "the Oval" and "sweets"—the question tends to be lost sight of altogether.

§5.43   Anselm's assertion that *"grammaticus"* signifies *grammatica* precisively, but is appellative of, refers to, men, brings to mind the doctrine of connotation and denotation (§4.3): "literate" could be said to "connote" literacy and to "denote" human beings. It should however be plain, from what has been said before, that Anselm displays much greater logical sophistication than do the purveyors of the distinction between connotation and denotation in the modern era: that distinction, as usually presented, constitutes a deterioration from his position. For instance, it would appear that he showed a sounder logical instinct in retaining the functor *"est"* and using the shock of *"grammaticus est grammatica"* than does J.S. Mill in preferring assertions such as " 'White' connotes whiteness", which in his system appears to leave open little possibility of an eventual intelligible connection with *de re* correlates. The sentences about connotation raise problems which *"grammaticus est grammatica"*, as explained by Anselm, and used by him as an inferential equivalent of *" 'grammaticus' significat (per se) grammaticam"* does not. Anselm's nonsense at least makes glaringly apparent the novelty of the semantical categories which are here involved; Mill's cognate assertions are restricted to the *de voce* mode in terms of "connotes", and hence tend to leave veiled the logically startling features of the situation. At the same time the distinction between precisive signification and reference, as presented by Anselm, will plainly serve to do justice to the contentions of both Joseph and Mill (§4.3), insofar as those contentions are just, on the topic of concrete and attributive terms.

VI

THE DOCTRINE OF *DE GRAMMATICO:*
THE LOGICAL CO-ORDINATES

§6.01   Up to this point the account of the problems of *De gram-matico* and of their development has been couched in terms of an *ad hoc* vocabulary which issues from many sources: language of a primarily pre-theoretical nature, translations of medieval Latin terminology, some of which has become embedded in current modes of expression in various misleading ways (e.g. "substance"), philosophical and logical terminology of the modern era, and so on. The aim of the present Section is to begin to state the doctrine of the dialogue, insofar as this is possible, in terms of a unitary vocabulary and syntax. The provision of a systematic language with an ample variety of parts of speech is a particularly pressing problem, as the philosophical Latin of Anselm's time had already acquired the facility of creating parts of speech belonging to semantical categories not ordinarily required for pre-theoretical purposes—a point of which Anselm was acutely conscious; the grammar of the language in terms of which the dialogue is described must hence match or exceed that of Anselm's Latin in its recognition of varieties of parts of speech, and it will become evident that the grammatical categories of everyday English do not fulfil this requirement. Again,

English is particularly unsuited for the provision of stable co-ordinates against which to measure the Latin text, since it displays idiosyncrasies, such as articles, which are altogether absent in the original: to rely entirely on English at least leaves open the possibility of the introduction of new difficulties arising from the peculiarities of this language—difficulties altogether foreign to the Latin discussion. One has only to consider the form in which the Theory of Descriptions was presented by Russell in order to realise this: he made the whole discussion centre around the word "the"—an orientation scarcely possible in a language like Latin, which contains no articles, definite or indefinite.

§6.02   There is at least one system of logic which appears capable of fulfilling the requirements adnumbrated in the preceding paragraph: it is that of the Polish logician S. Leśniewski, and in particular that part of it which he called "Ontology". It exhibits exactly that capacity for systematically excelling the already enriched medieval Latin in the multiplication of parts of speech which is so essential to the present project. This multiplication takes place within the framework of an axiomatised system which, thanks to its extreme flexibility, provides a sympathetic yet precise elucidation of some of the most difficult passages of the dialogue. Indeed, the task of elucidating such passages might well be adopted as a standard test of the *finesse* of a given logical system.

§6.03   Although Leśniewski's Ontology is to be adopted as a means of systematically exhibiting the logical articulations of *De grammatico*, the imposing symbolic apparatus in terms of which such an exhibition is effected does not automatically absolve one from a consideration of what may turn out to be the limitations of such an approach. Thus it might be urged that such an approach is wholly misplaced, insofar as it represents an attempt to express the thought of Anselm in a totally alien idiom. Again, the proposal results in the imposition on the given text of an interpretational hypothesis the propriety of which can never be guaranteed absolutely. Such objections are not without foundation, for it is doubtless all too easy, when armed with a powerful system of modern logic, to deal in

Procrustean fashion with the available data. However, to be conscious of possible limitations is already to be on one's guard against their consequences. Insofar as *De grammatico* in particular and medieval logic in general are concerned, I can only call attention to the indubitable sympathy of approach which exists between them and Ontology: this sympathy will, I hope, become amply evident as the examination advances, and may at the very least be regarded as yet another facet of that unity of spirit animating both modern and medieval logic of which historians have only in recent years become aware. I further venture to suggest that translation into English, and discussion solely in English, of the work in question (unless supported by a systematic background such as that of Ontology) could carry with it the risk of reproducing and extending, instead of solving, the interpretational difficulties which the dialogue raises, and this at least for the reasons suggested in §6.01: *Nil agit exemplum quod litem lite resolvit*, as Anselm would say (*De Casu Diaboli* 11, SI 248.8). Such translation and discussion already carry with them implicit interpretational hypotheses which not only prey upon their users in such a way as to be beyond the reach of precise, conscious, and explicit control, but are also liable to distort the coordinates of the original thought in such a way as to engender a species of pseudomorphism which renders them lost beyond recovery; the history of the histories of medieval thought in the modern era exhibits a case in point here.

§6.04   It now remains to outline the manner and extent of the application of Ontology for the purpose of analysing the statements which occur in *De grammatico*. Ontology proper, as will become apparent from §6.1 and §6.2, is a theory of objects in general, whereas most of the argument of the dialogue consists of discussions of particular sorts of objects, such as men, stones, horses, literates, whites, and so on. True, it is quite plain that use of terms referring to such objects is intended to be purely exemplary, and that generalisation thereon is assumed to be possible (1.000, 4.2415, 4.82); yet the fact still remains, because of the particularity mentioned, that theories or fragments of theories of particular sorts of objects are encountered in the text. How, then, can Ontology be brought to bear on the text? It has already been remarked how prolific Ontology is in parts of speech. This feature will in fact prove to be highly valuable in elucidating sentences which occur in the dialogue, notwithstanding the fact that those sentences contain names belonging to theories which are not themselves part of Ontology. However, reference to Ontological norms, or the use of parts of speech pertaining to Ontology, plainly does not make the sentences validated, or those in which such parts of speech occur, into sentences of Ontology. The latter has its own axioms, but the axioms for the theories which incorporate non-Ontological names such as "man", "horse", and so on, are wanting. Two points should hence be noted: (i) theses involving names of the sort mentioned, or abbreviations for such names, are not theses of Ontology, notwithstanding the appearance of parts of speech explicated in Ontology within those theses; (ii) the manner in which the truth of such theses is to be accounted for has to be considered. Anselm assumes that everyone is capable on reflection of disengaging these of the theories of familiar constant terms from their pre-theoretical background (3.800), and this assumption will be taken over for the purposes of the analyses presented, i.e. such theories will be assumed to exist and to be given.

§6.1 *Ontology: formal and informal background*

§6.11 In this and the following sections at least some elementary acquaintance with the modern versions of logic, and in particular with the Calculus of Propositions and the notion of Quantification, is desirable.

For, according to Leśniewski, a necessary preliminary to Ontology is Protothetic, which embraces what are ordinarily described under the headings mentioned. Ampler details of Ontology may be found in *LR* on which much of what now follows is based; references to theses of *LR* will be made by means of the numbers which they bear in that work, which are invariably preceded by "T".

§6.12 The theses of Ontology present truths as to how things are (*LR*153); hereunder they are to be symbolically formulated in the

Peano-Russell style, i.e. they will be primarily articulated in terms of those functors whose arguments are propositions, e.g. "$\sim$" for "it is not the case that", "$.$" for "and", "$\vee$" for the non-exclusive "or", "$\supset$" for "if......then......", and "$\equiv$" for "if and only if". Such functors can form functions by composition with unanalysed *propositional* variables ("p", "q", "r", etc.) as their arguments, as in "$p \supset q$" ("if p then q"); since propositions are either true or false, such functions are sometimes said to be "truth-functions"—a notion with which Boethius was familiar. However, the theses of Ontology are secondarily articulated in terms of those functors whose arguments are *names*: *nominal* variables for such arguments will be drawn from the lower-case italicised letters "a", "b", "c", etc. Thus "ε" ("is" or "is a") is a functor which takes names as arguments, as in "$a \varepsilon b$" ("a) is (a) b"): the function thus formed, being propositional, can then itself serve as argument to a functor which takes propositions as its arguments, giving a case such as "$a \varepsilon b . \equiv . a \varepsilon b$" ("$a$ is a b if and only if a is a b") ($LR160$). The punctuation of sentences compounded in this way will be external to the propositional functions, and will correspond roughly to the bracketing which is familiar in common algebra; it will be effected by means of dots and clusters of dots, the strengths of which vary, in the first place, directly as the number of dots: the scope of n dots adjoining a propositional functor other than "$.$" extends outwards on the side of the expression corresponding to the side of the functor on which the n dots occur, and is only terminated by the end of the expression or by a cluster of $>n$ dots; the scope of n dots immediately following a quantifier (e.g. "[$\exists a$]" or "[a]", cf. §6.20) extends to its right and only terminates when $>n$ dots are reached, or when n dots occur immediately preceding a propositional functor other than "$.$"; n dots which act as a conjunction ("$.$", "and") between two propositional expressions have scope in both directions until n or $>n$ dots are reached ($LR160$ - 161). The quantifiers mentioned are read off, "for some $a, b \ldots$" ("[$\exists \ a \ b \ldots$]") and "for all $a, b \ldots$" ("[$a \ b \ldots$] "); (cf. $LR160$ and §6.20). The lower case Greek letters "φ", "ψ", etc. will be used as variables for *predicates*, where a predicate is, roughly speaking, a propositional function with one or more of its arguments omitted; predicate variables will be quantified in the same manner as nominal variables. English approximations to some sentences constructed in the manner described are provided in §6.2 below.

§6.13   The single primitive term, namely "ε", which figures in the single axiom (§6.21.1) of Ontology on which Leśniewski's system was based in 1920 may now be introduced (*LR*163). It should be noted that this introduction is not part of the system: any mode of introduction which is effective will serve, be it diagram, verbal description, or any other pre-systematic activity. In this spirit one may describe the functor "ε" as a proposition-forming functor each of the two arguments of which is a name or name-like expression: a proposition of the form "*a* ε *b*" is true if and only if, *either* "*a*" and "*b*" name the same individual object and no others, *or* "*a*" names an individual object and no others and "*b*" names several such objects, one of which is *a*. A most precise example of a verb corresponding to the functor "ε" in a "natural" language is the Latin "*est*" as it occurs in sentences such as "*Socrates est Socrates*" and "*Socrates est philosophus*"; in English "Barkis is willin'" or "The present Queen of England is regal" will serve as examples. Should difficulties as to the exact import of this functor still subsist in the minds of those to whom it is being introduced, then only the individual or cumulative effect of the collection of hints, examples, and cases, or of any other activity which serves to show the meaning of "ε" (or of whichever functor is chosen as primitive) can be resorted to in the first place; this first inkling, which it is to be hoped the description and examples given above have already provided, can then be progressively deepened by fuller appreciation, if this is necessary, as the development of the system proceeds. In his writings on Ontology Leśniewski used capital letters as the variables (nominal) preceding the "ε" in those cases where the context made it clear that reference to only one individual was intended; however, this distinction is purely stylistic; it may on occasion add to the perspicuity of an expression, but at the same time might lead the unwary reader to imagine that it was indicative of a diversity of semantical category, whereas this is not so. For the purposes of the present exposition, therefore, lower case nominal (proper or common) variables are used throughout.

§6.2   *Ontology: Quantification, Axiom, and Definitions.*

§6.20   Sentences framed in the language of Ontology incorporate, as has been remarked (§6.12) the signs used as variables enclosed in square brackets, such signs being sometimes preceded by " ∃ ", so that when nominal variables are in question, one has "[*abc* . . .]" or "[∃ *abc* . . .]"; these are to be read off as "for all *a, b, c,* . . ." and "for some *a, b, c,* . . . "respectively, and are known as "quantifiers". In the expositions which follow, quantifiers for variables other than name-variables will occasionally be used. However, as those governing name-variables have a most prominent part to play, only these will now be discussed in any detail. It is highly important to realise that the name-variables which are to be used are variables for *any* name or name-like expression (including the grammarian's adjectives) whether empty (i.e. having no referent(s)) or non-empty (i.e. having referents). Further, the non-empty expressions may either designate one object only (in which case they are unshared nominal expressions — "proper names", "definite descriptions") or may designate more than one object (in which case they are shared nominal expressions—"common names"). Finally, expressions of this nominal nature may be simple or compound, i.e. may either be expressions of which no part is a name (e.g. "Socrates", "man") or expressions parts of which retain their separate identity as names (e.g. "the present King of France"). From the last example it is clear that what Russell called "definite descriptions" count as nominal expressions for the purposes of Ontology. Remarks analogous to those just made could be framed in respect of predicate-expressions (symbolised by "φ", "ψ" . . . . . .); such predicate-expressions are those forms of words which, when completed by one or more nominal expressions, form propositions. Quantifications of the sorts described range over *expressions* of appropriate semantical category (e.g. names) as opposed to whatever is named by such expressions, or for which the expressions stand; there hence arise no problems of the sort which face Quine in Q when quantification is extended to predicates. At the same time such quantification must not be taken to make the sentences in which it occurs into metalinguistic assertions.

§6.21   The following is the single axiom on which Leśniewski's Ontology was originally based (1920):

.1 $[ab] :: a\varepsilon b . \equiv : . [\exists c] . c\varepsilon a : . [c] : c\varepsilon a . \supset . c\varepsilon b:.$
$[cd] : c\varepsilon a . d\varepsilon a . \supset . c\varepsilon d$ (LRT34)

i.e. for all a and b : a is b if and only if for some c, c is a,
and for all c, if c is a then c is b, and for all c and d, if c
is a and d is a then c is d.

Considerable reductions in length have since been shown to be possible (LR163-4). "ε" is the only Ontological functor which figures in .1; it has nominal variables as its arguments, while all the other functors ("$\equiv$", "$\supset$", ".") are propositional, i.e. take propositions or propositional functions as their arguments. Cross-references to sources, justifications, definitions, or correlated material will be placed after numbered sentences, as in the case of .1 above; thus, after .1, T34 of LR is acknowledged as a source.

§6.22   A full and complete exposition of Ontology would require that the rules of definition appropriate to the various types of definition used, should be explicitly stated (LR172-5). However, for the present it suffices to say that definitions introduce new expressions which have not yet occurred in the system in question, by reference to expressions which have already occurred. Further remarks will be added as the definitions are presented below. First come definitions of proposition-forming functors having one argument which is a name. (The description given in this last sentence is of the *semantical category*, or "part of speech" of these *definienda*):

.1 $[a] : ex(a) . \equiv . [\exists b] . b \varepsilon a$ (LR T1)
i.e., for all a, there exists at least one a if and only if for some b, b is
    a . (First functor of existence).

.2 $[a] : sol(a) . \equiv : [b\ c]: b \varepsilon a . c \varepsilon a . \supset . b\varepsilon c$ (LR T5)
i.e., for all a, there exists at most one a if and only if for all b and c,
    if b is a and c is a, then b is c . (Second functor of existence).

.3 $[a] : \mathrm{ob}(a) . \equiv . [\exists b] . a \, \varepsilon \, b$ (*LR* T16)

i.e., for all a, there exists exactly one a if and only if for some b, a is b . (Third functor of existence).

Next follow some definitions of proposition-forming functors each of which has two names as arguments:

.4 $[ab] : . a \subset b . \equiv : [c] : c \, \varepsilon \, a . \supset . c \, \varepsilon \, b$ (*LR* T19)

i.e., for all a and b, all a is b if and only if for all c, if c is a then c is b . (Weak inclusion).

.5 $[ab] : . a \not\subset b . \equiv : [c] : c \, \varepsilon \, a . \supset . \sim (c \, \varepsilon \, b)$ (*LR* T23)

i.e., for all a and b, no a is b if and only if for all c, if c is a then it is not the case that c is b. . (Weak exclusion).

.6 $[ab] : a \triangle b . \equiv . [\exists c] . c \, \varepsilon \, a . c \, \varepsilon \, b$ (*LR* T20)

i.e., for all a and b, some a is b if and only if for some c, c is a and c is b . (Partial inclusion).

.7 $[ab] : a \not\triangle b . \equiv . [\exists c] . c \, \varepsilon \, a . \sim (c \, \varepsilon \, b)$ (*LR* T24)

i.e., for all a and b, some a is-not b if and only if for some c, c is a and it is not the case that c is b . (Partial exclusion) .

.8 $[ab] : a = b . \equiv . a \, \varepsilon \, b . b \, \varepsilon \, a$ (*LR* T25)

i.e., for all a and b, a is the same object as b if and only if a is b and b is a . (Singular identity) .

.9 $[ab] : a \circ b . \equiv : [c] : c \, \varepsilon \, a .$

i.e., for all a and b, only all a is b if and only if for all c, c is a if and only if c is b . (Weak identity) .

.10 $[a \, b] : : a \square b . \equiv : . [\exists c] . c \, \varepsilon \, a : . [c] : c \, \varepsilon \, a . \equiv . c \, \varepsilon \, b$ (*LR* T26)

i.e., for all a and b, only every a is b if and only if for some c, c is a and for all c, c is a if and only if c is b . (Strong identity) .

All the definitions so far given are Prothetical definitions, since they introduce functors belonging to the semantical category of *proposition*-forming functors. However, the definition of "trm$< >$" which now follows is an *Ontological* definition (*LR*173–5), since its *definiendum*, being an argument of "ε", for instance, is *nominal* in nature; in fact the semantical category of "trm$< >$" may be speci-

fied thus: it is a functor which forms a *name* from a proposition-
forming functor (i.e. from "φ"), the latter taking one name as its
argument to form a proposition:

.11 $[a\varphi] : a \, \varepsilon \, \mathrm{trm}{<}\varphi{>} \, . \equiv . \, a \, a\varepsilon \, a \, . \, \varphi \, (a)$

i.e., for all a and φ, a is a term satisfying φ if and only if a is a and
φ of a.

The angular and other types of brackets used in .11, as well as in
.12-.15, and .17 (below) serve as marks of the diverse semantical
categories to which the various functors defined belong. In .11 a
name ("trm$<\varphi>$") is formed from a verb ("φ"): thus if "φ" is
"leads", then "trm$<\varphi>$" is "leader" . However, it is also possible
to perform the reverse process, i.e. to form verbs from names. Thus,
reverting now to Protothetical definition, one has:

.12 $[ab] : \varepsilon \, \{b\} \, (a) \, . \equiv . \, a \, \varepsilon \, b$

Here, from the name "b", the verb "$\varepsilon\{b\}$" is framed, so that, for
instance, if "b" is "deputy", then "$\varepsilon\{b\}$" is "deputises." The "$\varepsilon\{\ \}$"
defined by .12 is a functor-forming functor for one argument which
is a name, the functor thus formed being a proposition-forming
functor for one nominal argument. Of course, "natural" languages
do not always display the verb-noun correlation which .11 and .12
guarantee for the language of Ontology: the "barbaric" proliferation
of abstract names in the Latin of medieval philosophers was part
of an attempt to ensure a similar, but not the same, guarantee. Two
other functors of the same semantical category as "$\varepsilon\{\ \}$" may also
be defined:

.13 $[ab] : \subset\{a\}(b) \, . \equiv . \, b \subset a$
.14 $[ab] : \mathrm{Cl}\{a\}(b) \, . \equiv . \, b \circ a$

There are various ways of expressing the intention of these two
definitions: thus "$\subset\{a\}$" could be rendered as, "form an aggre-
gate of a's", and "Cl $\{a\}$" as, "form the class of a's"; alternatively
the first could be said to define "being included in a", and the
second to define "to be a" in certain contexts (cf.§6.311). The second
will be found to play a most important part in elucidating one of

Anselm's uses of *"esse"* . Now verbs (predicates), including those which have just been defined, may themselves be arguments of an "is", as in "To walk is to move" (*APH*56, cf. *APH*54,55,96); hence a proposition-forming functor which takes such verbs as arguments is required; such a functor, although typographically and phonetically indistinguishable in pre-theoretical language from the "is" which, like "ε", has two nominal arguments, will nevertheless be of a semantical category differing from that of "ε". This difference should strictly speaking be marked by a difference in brackets, but is assumed to be sufficiently obvious from the diversity of argument-signs, as in the definition of the "ε" which takes verbs as arguments, thus:

.15 $\quad [\varphi\psi] : : \varphi \, \varepsilon \, \psi \, . \, \equiv : . \, [\, \exists \, a \,] : \varphi(a) \, . \, \psi(a) : . \, [b] :$
$\varphi(b) \, . \, \equiv . \, a \circ b$

The "ε" herein defined will be referred to as a "higher order" ε , in order to distinguish it from the primitive "lower order" ε which takes nominal arguments. Boethius shows himself aware of the differing semantical possibilities of "is" (*"est"*) by distinguishing between the "is" of "Cicero is healthy" and that of *"man* is *animal"* (where *"man"* is used to "refer" to the species (*BC*201A-202A)); these two uses correspond exactly to the lower and higher ε respectively. Given .15, all definitions and theses in which the lower order "ε" figures have their isomorphs in terms of the higher order "ε" (*LA*248-9). Thus, corresponding to .8 a singular identity having as arguments not names, but verbs, can now be defined:

.16 $\quad [\varphi\psi] : \varphi = \psi \, . \, \equiv . \, \varphi \, \varepsilon \, \psi \, . \, \psi \, \varepsilon \, \varphi$

Here, as in .15, it is assumed that the nature of the argument-signs is sufficient to call attention to the fact that the semantical category of the *definiendum* of .16 differs from that of the *definiendum* of .8. Given, therefore, definitions of the type exemplified in .12-.14, which are said to define "many-link functors", and the further functors definable once .15 is available, a language rich in new parts of speech, and capable of accurately delineating diversities which are slurred over in pre-theoretical speech, is seen to be possible.

Thus, combining the *definiendum* of an Ontological definition (.11) with that of a protothetical one (.14), one can define:

.17 $[a_\varphi]$:Cl$\{_{\varphi}\}$ (a) . $\equiv$. Cl$\{$trm$<\varphi>\}$ (a)

Here "Cl$\{$ $\}$" is a proposition-forming functor for one nominal argument, that functor being defined in terms of a name-forming functor (i.e. "trm$< >$") which forms a name from a one (nominal) argument proposition-forming functor ("φ"). The description just given is already an index of the extreme subtlety and variety of parts of speech which can now be constructed, exactly as required in §6.01. The following Ontological definitions should also be noted:

.18 $[a]$: $a\ \varepsilon\ \bigvee$. $\equiv$. $a\ \varepsilon\ a$ (LR T72)

.19 $[a]$: $a\ \varepsilon\ \bigwedge$. $\equiv$. $a\ \varepsilon\ a$. $\sim$ $(a\ \varepsilon\ a)$ (LR T73)

In .18 the *definiendum* may be read "*a* is an object", and in .19 as "*a* is an object which does not exist". It will also be useful to have available the functor "$\cap$" ("product", "and") at two levels, nominal and functorial, thus:—

.20 $[a\ b\ c]$: $a\ \varepsilon\ b\cap c$. $\equiv$. $a\ \varepsilon\ b$. $a\ \varepsilon\ c$

.21 $[\varphi\ \psi\ \chi]$: $\varphi\ \varepsilon\ \psi\cap\chi$. $\equiv$. $\varphi\ \varepsilon\ \psi$. $\varphi\ \varepsilon\ \chi$

There will also be occasions on which the difference between nominal negation (defined below) and the propositional negation available in Protothetic, will have some bearing on the discussion:

.22 $[a\ b]$: $a\ \varepsilon\ \diagup\!\!\!\sim\ (b)$. $\equiv$. $a\ \varepsilon\ a$. $\sim$ $(a\ \varepsilon\ b)$ (LR T74)

Although this outline is only a sketch of the beginnings of the topic, it will in fact be found that the definitions so far given will be sufficient for most of the present project.

§6.221   Lest it should be supposed that §6.22.4 and §6.22.7 commit Ontology to a particular position as regards the categorical propositions of syllogistic, the following forms of inclusion and exclusion should also be noted:

.1 $[a\ b]$: : $a\ \sqsubset\ b$. $\equiv$: . $[\exists c]$. $c\ \varepsilon\ a$: . $[c]$: $c\ \varepsilon\ a$. $\supset$. $c\ \varepsilon\ b$
        (LR T18)

.2 $\quad [a\ b] :: a \not\subset b \ . \ \equiv \ : \ . \ [\exists c] \ . \ c \ \varepsilon \ a : \ . \ [c] : c \ \varepsilon \ a \ . \ \supset \ .$
$$\sim (c \ \varepsilon \ b) \qquad\qquad (LR\ T22)$$
.1 defines strong inclusion (to be read "every a is b"); .2 defines strong exclusion (to be read "every a is-not b") (cf. LR157).

§6.222 *De grammatico*, in common with so much of medieval logical literature, uses constant terms as representatives of classes of terms, instead of introducing a special type of variable for each of those classes. The dialogue's own title betokens this habit: "*grammaticus*" is quite explicitly a specimen paronym, and the results of the dialogue are taken to apply to all paronyms. In order to present succinct formulations of the sentences used in the dialogue it will be necessary to abbreviate the constant terms which occur in those sentences. This device will facilitate excursions into the theories of the constant terms in question. At the same time, bearing in mind the presupposed possibilities of generalisation which they carry with them, those terms may be regarded as variables capable of instantiation by other terms of the same class. The abbreviations which are to be used for names are as follows:

.1 "g" for "*grammaticus*"

.2 "h" for "*homo*"

.3 "l" for "*lapis*"

.4 "r" for "*rationalis*"

.5 "a" for "*animal*"

.6 "m" for "*mortalis*"

.7 "w" for "*albus*"

These constant-name abbreviations are expressed in heavy type in order to distinguish them from name-variables. Translations from Latin into English and *vice-versa* will be assumed to be given, so that discussion of the text can take place using the English versions of the names which are abbreviated in .1 to .7 above. These versions are, respectively, "literate", "man", "stone", "rational", "animal", "mortal", and "white". In addition, the lower-case Greek letters which figure in the following list will be reserved for the abstract names shown:

.8   "γ" for "*grammatica*"

.9   "λ" for "*rationalitas*"

.10   " $\propto$ " for "*rationalitas et mortalitas et animalitas*"

.11   "ω" for "*albedo*"

The compound abstract abbreviated at .10 is equivalent to "*human-itas*" .

§6.3   *Theses and Antitheses*

§6.301   In all his works, including the dialogue at present under consideration, Saint Anselm is at pains to underline the necessity of understanding the true logical form of an utterance, as opposed to its apparent, overt, or merely grammatical form (3.33, SI 188*n*, SI 235.10.12, SI 253.19.22, SII 49.8.13). It is in exactly this spirit that the present section is undertaken. As a preliminary, the Anselmian usages of *esse, essentia* etc. (§6.31) and the status of key-terms for his definitions (§6.32) will be located. The exact semantical status of the main theses can then be precisely determined (as well as that of the antitheses) and the general course of the dialogue sketched in the light of these decisions (§6.33). Finally, elucidations of subsidiary arguments will be appended (§6.34).

§6.31   *Identification of some of the functors used by Anselm:*

§6.311   "*esse*", "*intelligere*", and "*res*"

§6.3111   The dialogue contains references to the *esse* of such things as men, animals, and literates; in such cases this infinitive ("*esse*") is followed by the genitive of the appropriate names (e.g. "*esse hominis*", "*esse grammatici*" (3.431)): the *prima facie* translation of such words into English would be by means of such phrases as "to be man", "being man", or even "the being of a man". Now the text asserts that the *esse* of anything is given in its definition (3.-800), and that to say that the *esse* of one thing is not the *esse* of another amounts to saying that they are not defined in the same way (3.431, 3.44, 3.901, 4.24). From this it is clear that to talk about the *esse* of a thing is, for Anselm, to talk about its definitional or quasi-definitional equivalentiality (if one may so attempt to express it). In terms of Ontology, the notion here in question may be expressed in the following fashion: to every name or name-like expression "*a*" there corresponds a proposition-forming functor "Cl{*a*}", itself formed from that name or name-like expression, and defined as follows:

.1   [*a b*] : Cl{*a*}(*b*) . ≡ . *b* ○ *a*   (§6.22.14)

The functor here defined is in the fact the counterpart of the infinitive verbal form derived from, or corresponding to, the name "*a*" in certain contexts of pre-theoretical language; e.g. if "*a*" is "defendant", then "Cl{*a*}" is the "to defend" of a sentence such as "To defend is to uphold", or if "*a*" is "*dux*" then "Cl{*a*}" is the "*ducere*" in a sentence such as "*Ducere est imperare*". In a logical language such as that of Ontology, the creation of such an infinitive is effected quite simply in terms of .1, but in pre-theoretical language such infinitives do not always exist; in the absence of a logical symbolic language, therefore, some medieval logicians formed the required infinitives by the use of "*esse*" and the genitive of the name in question, as in the examples encountered above.

§6.3112   For the purpose of constructing an infinitive from English names, "to" with the termination "-ise" would serve; "man" would give "to man-ise", "white" "to white-ise", and so on. This is less ambiguous than the more usual "to be (a) man", "being man", and so on, although the latter at least avoid the impression given by the genitive in the Latin form that the *esse* of a thing is itself a thing in a familiar, lower-order, sense of "thing".

§6.3113 It is plain that the "*est*" which has proposition-forming functors of the type of "Cl{ }" as its arguments (as in the case of "*esse grammatici non est esse hominis*") is not the same functor as the "*est*" which has names as its arguments (as in "*Socrates est albus*"). The difference here in question was noted by both Boethius (*BDIL*309B—310C) and Aquinas (*APH*96, cf. *APH*54,55,56) when they commented on Aristotle's *De Interpretatione* (16[b] 20). It will in fact be found that the definition already proffered, namely:

.1 $[\varphi\,\psi] :\,: \varphi\,\varepsilon\,\psi \,.\,\equiv\,:\,.\,[\,\exists\,a]\,:\,.\,\varphi\,(a)\,.\,\psi\,(a)\,:\,.\,[b]\,:\,\varphi(b)\,.$
$$\equiv\,.\,a \circ b \qquad\qquad (\S6.22.15)$$

represents the first of these two sorts of *"est"* . Thus, using "Cl $\langle g \rangle$" and "Cl$\langle h \rangle$" for the "φ" and "ψ" of the left-hand side of .1, and negating the result, one has:

.2 $\sim (\mathrm{Cl}\langle g \rangle\,\varepsilon\,\mathrm{Cl}\langle h \rangle)$

as the analysis of the Latin sentence mentioned first in this paragraph. Incidentally, it may well be that the use of *"fulgor"* and *"splendor"* at 3.540 represents an attempt to give a concrete illustration which is to some extent isomorphic in sense with a situation such as that analysed in .2

§6.3114 The connection between the *"esse"* of a thing and its definition, noted above, in turn leads to two other associated notions, namely those of *intelligere* and *significare*. The connection between understanding (*intelligere*) and *esse* is set up at 3.41, 3.42, where the meaning of sentences 3.310 and 3.311, both of which involve the expression "can be understood to be", is said to be equatable with statements involving *esse*. The connection between meaning (*significatio*) and understanding (*intelligere*) is plain from the opening of 3.21, where a counter-example to certain inferences involving *intelligi* is developed from the signification of the name "animal". It is hence clear that analysis of sentences involving *intelligere* could at least to some extent be carried out at the level of language suggested above in respect of *esse*-statements. The relation between *esse*-statements and statements of meaning (*significatio*) becomes plain at 4.602 and 4.603, where the distinction between the *de voce* and *de re* modes of expressing the dialogue's findings is made quite explicit: in the *de voce* mode one expresses the meaning of the name in question, whereas in the *de re* mode one shows the thing (*res*) which is in question when the name is being used. For example "literate" is said to signify a quality (literacy), and this is the *de voce* expression of the *de re* truth "*Literate* is a quality (literacy)", the later being analysable in terms of the higher-order "ε" encountered in the last paragraph. As far as the text itself goes this parallelism between *de voce* and *de re* modes of expression may appear to commit Anselm to a crude theory of meaning according to which a name has meaning by standing for a thing (*res*) in the way that "Socrates" has meaning by standing for Socrates, and his statement at 4.5143 that words have meaning only in respect of things (*voces non significant nisi res*) might seem to underline this *prima facie* crudity. However, the distinction between precisive signification and reference given at 4.232–4.2341 is already sufficient to deliver Anselm from such a charge, and the suggestions already made and still to be made as to the level of language (and hence the sense of *res*) at which the *de re* versions of the discussion move will further make clear that he is concerned to avoid just the crudity now in question. Indeed, it is apparent that for him, as also for Ontology, a word like "thing" is not univocal, but is to be correlated with the sense of *ens* which happens to be in question. In fact the medieval doctrine that words like *ens, res, unum,* and *aliquid* are non-univocal is here being exploited by Anselm. For Ontology the many senses of each of these can be defined in terms of successive senses of "ε" obtainable by carrying on the process initiated at §6.22.15 to higher levels. The difficulties which arise in modern logic when a word like "thing" is taken to be univocal may be seen in all their force in the troubles experienced by Quine in quantification theory, and so lucidly revealed by him in the various essays of *Q*.

§6.3115 In order that the modern tendency to attribute a univocal sense to "thing" may not constitute a bar to the understanding of Anselm's text, the word "*res*" has been translated as "circumstance" at appropriate points (e.g. 4.5142, 4.603, 4.604).

§6.312 *Abstract names,* essentia, *and participles.*

§6.3121 It has already been remarked that "*grammatica*" must be translated in such a way that its status as an abstract noun is obvious, i.e. as "literacy" (§4.2). There occur in the dialogue expressions such as "that which has the essence of literate" ("*qui habet essentiam grammatici*") (3.701). The question of how such abstract nouns, and phrases containing them or a mention of "essence", are to be rendered in the language of Ontology will first be considered. The dual interpretation of participles suggested in §5.322 will then be investigated.

§6.3122   Since it is still possible, in English, to speak of *literacy* being predicated of something, this being an allowable alternative to saying that "is literate" is predicated of that thing, it therefore seems feasible to consider such abstract names in relation to verbs or functors. It will be found that the following definition of "trm-$<\varphi>$" (i.e. "term satisfying φ") serves as a framework for Anselm's uses of verbs in general, as well as some of his uses of abstract words:

.1 $[a_\varphi] : a \ \varepsilon \ \text{trm}<\varphi> \ . \ \equiv \ . \ a \ \varepsilon \ a \ . \ \varphi \ (a)$ (§6.22.11)

Two of Anselm's examples serve to elucidate the general intention of .1; thus, if "φ" is "*lucet*" then "trm $<\varphi>$" is "*lucens*" (understood nominally), since he would be prepared to equate "a *lucet*" with "a *lucens est*" (*Monologion* 6, SI 20.14). In this case the nominally understood participle "*lucens*" names whatever satisfies the functor "*lucet*". Likewise, he equates "*habet*" with "*habens est*" (4.8121). This kind of equation represents the familiar transformation, which Aristotle and Boethius mention, of predications *de secundo adiacente* into predications *de tertio adiacente* (BDIL349A). Within the range of substitutions for "φ" lie abstract nouns, so that from "literacy (is predicated) of a" (a case of "$\varphi(a)$") one can derive "term satisfying 'literacy'" (a case of "trm $<\varphi>$") in accordance with .1 . The expression given to cases of this sort by Anselm varies immensely, but the general pattern which emerges is as follows: instead of saying that *literacy* is predicated of a, he would say that a has literacy ("a *habet grammaticam*") . However, since "*habet*", as just mentioned, is equated with "*habens est*", therefore "a *habet grammaticam*" becomes "a *est habens grammaticam*" (4.24120; cf. *Monologion* 16) : this is a clear enough case of the formation of a name-like expression ("*habens grammaticam*") from an abstract noun ("*grammatica*"). Sometimes a participle other than "*habens*" is used (e.g. 4.24120). The Latin participial forms which thus constitute cases of "trm$<\varphi>$" must usually be regarded as nominal arguments for proposition-forming functors whose arguments are names. However, as Priscian remarks, participles can be either name-like or verb-like (*KII* 551.8.10); this latter aspect—the verbal facet of participles and participial forms—will be treated in §6.3125 below. Priscian treats of name-verb relations, and speaks of denominative verbs, in his *Partitiones* (*KII* 432.18–434.15, *KIII* 479.-1.3).

§6.3123 However, it is quite clear that participles and expressions formed from abstract names and participles are not the only correlates of "trm$< >$" as defined in §6.3122.1. Thus, provided that "*habens grammaticam*" is understood as a name, then "*habens grammaticam*" can be replaced by "*qui habet essentiam grammatici*" (3.701) or "*aliquid habens grammaticam*" (4.801). Anselm, it will be recalled, supposed that the range of abstract names here in play would serve to delimit the class of shared names other than substance names; the relativity of such a notion, even in the Middle Ages, has already been described (§4.10). For after Anselm, abstract names were introduced practically whenever required, so that each shared name could in principle have its abstract correlate. However, even this elasticity is easily matched in Ontology by the formation of verbs from names (i.e. the converse of the process represented by §6.3122.1) in accordance with the following definition:

.1 $[ab]$: $\varepsilon\{b\}(a)$. $\equiv$. $a \, \varepsilon \, b$ (§6.22.12)

For example, if "*b*" is "lux", then "$\varepsilon\{b\}$" represents the corresponding verb, namely "*lucet*", i.e. "*lucens est*". In those cases where the name "*b*" has no such available verbal correlate in pre-theoretical language, it would be possible to create one in accordance with the principles outlined above, by use of the participle and abstract noun, so that "*est sciens grammaticam*" would then be the verbal correlate of "*grammaticus*".

§6.3124 Hence, given "*grammatica*" as a supposedly primitive abstract name, "trm$<\gamma>$" could be introduced by means of §6.-3122.1, thus:

.1 $[a] : a \; \varepsilon \; \mathrm{trm}<\gamma> \; . \; \equiv \; . \; a \; \varepsilon \; a \; . \; \gamma \; (a)$

So that, following the general pattern of paronymy as conceived by the ancients (cf. §4.1) *"grammaticus"* itself could next be introduced:

.2 $[a] : a \; \varepsilon \; \mathrm{g} \; . \; \equiv \; . \; a \; \varepsilon \; \mathrm{trm}<\gamma>$

This last expression is itself a particular case of the following:

.3 $[a \, b] : . \; [\, \exists \, \varphi] : a \; \varepsilon \; b \; . \; \equiv \; . \; a \; \varepsilon \; \mathrm{trm}<\varphi>$

"trm$<\varphi>$" of .3 could be interpreted by Anselm as "that which has the essence of *b*" in those cases where "*b*" was not paronymous in his sense (cf. 3.701). For the later medievals, *"habens* b-*eitas"* (where "b-*eitas*" is understood to be a value of "φ") would always be made available if "*b*" had no natural abstract correlate. The reciprocal relation between names and names formed from verbs shown in .3, and which is made universally possible, in the absence of other resources, by using "$\varepsilon \{ \; \}$" as a value of "φ" in accordance with the doctrine of §6.3123, has as its counterpart the Stoic notion of "reciprocal appellations" (*K*II 549).

§6.3125 Thus far, the participial forms encountered in the dialogue have been considered insofar as they are *nominal* in character, and the abstract names associated with them have been assumed to be either primitive or structured like the "$\varepsilon \{ \; \}$" of §6.3123. However, in §5.322 the special aptness of the use of a participial form such as *"sciens grammaticam"* in order to define a paronym such as "literate" was suggested, in that it would appear that such a form can function either as a name (corresponding to "trm$<\gamma>$") and hence a possible argument of the lower-order "ε", or as a functor (corresponding to "Cl$\{$trm$<\gamma>\}$") which could be an argument of the higher-order "ε". Now *sciens grammaticam"* is certainly used as a name in assertions such as *"omne sciens grammaticam est grammaticum"* (4.-2412). This could hence be interpreted as:

.1 $\mathrm{trm}<\gamma> \subset \mathrm{g}$

This nominal interpretation agrees well enough with Priscian's equation of *faciens eloquentem* with *qui facit eloquentem* (KIII 160.13). The thesis suggested in §5.322 is that although the "*sciens grammaticam*" of "*omne sciens grammaticam est grammaticum*" can be interpreted as "$\mathrm{trm} < \gamma >$", and hence as a name, nevertheless the "*sciens grammaticam*" with which we are concerned when a definition is being stated falls over on the verbal, predicative, side, as opposed to the nominal, and hence is to be interpreted as "$\mathrm{Cl}\{\mathrm{trm} < \gamma > \}$". And although, in the absence of more complete logical analyses it is probably fruitless to attach too much significance to the details of Priscian's uses of terms such as "name" and "verb" which occur both in grammatical and logical contexts, it may nevertheless be of some advantage to pass, *via* a more general remark of his, into an examination of those features of Anselm's text which support the thesis outlined in §5.322.

§6.3126 Thus, from what Priscian has to say about the general nature of participial forms, their dual nature becomes apparent: *Itaque cum et verbi quaedam sua prohibet hoc esse nomen, id est tempora et significationes, et nominis propria prohibent esse verbum, id est genera et casus .... mansit participium medium inter nomen et verbum. Unde rationabiliter hoc nomen est ei a grammaticis inditum per confirmationem duarum partium orationis principalium* (KII 551.4.10); *participia tam nominum quam verborum sibi defendunt structuram* (KIII 159.14.15; cf. KIII 565.6.7, 473.4, 486.28). Now Anselm had certainly studied Latin participles sufficiently to be able to give a precise account of the way in which they are used in certain cases (*De Veritate* 12, SI 196.13.18; cf. KII 565.11.24, KIII 487.19.25). There appears to be no reason, therefore, why Anselm should not appreciate the verbal, predicative, or functorial possibilities of *sciens grammaticam* and like forms; indeed, the position of this result in the dialogue as a whole (4.31), and everything he has to say about it, point to such an appreciation. In the first place there is the method by means of which he obtained this participial expression as the definition of *grammaticus*: the "*sciens grammaticam*" in question is that of "*homo sciens grammaticam*", but with "*homo*" struck out, i.e. "......*sciens gram-*

maticam" gives an accurate impression of what exactly is meant
(4.3). Secondly, although the Tutor of the dialogue says that
"signifying *sciens grammaticam*" amounts to "signifying *grammatica*" (4.31), he does not go on to remove the scandal against *usus
loquendi* constituted by "*grammaticus est grammatica*" (4.4341) in
a way which might appear obvious, i.e. by re-writing the sentence
defining *grammaticus* as "*grammaticus est sciens grammaticam*".
Instead, he persists in asserting that "*grammaticus est grammatica*"
has a place in logical assertions (4.5022, 4.5122) and that the
scandal serves to bring out differences in types of statement (4.62).
Nor can *sciens grammaticam* itself be explained away as an unim-
portant stop-gap result, destined only to lead lamely on to the conclusion that "*grammaticus*" signifies *grammatica,* since this same
result is later taken up as *habens grammaticam* (4.700) and extended in the example of *habens albedinem* (4.710). It is therefore
an important result, and yet is not used to make a fairly obvious
substitution which would have done away with the discrepancy
between the talk to which logic commits logicians and the talk
recognisable as sensible by ordinary folk. The reason behind this
refusal to substitute can only be that it could have led readers to
suppose that "*sciens grammaticam*" was here used as a name in a
sense certainly consonant with ordinary grammar in the way that
"*sciens grammaticam*" in "*Omne sciens grammaticam est grammaticum*" has earlier been used. It is as a part of speech falling over
on the verbal, and not the nominal, side of participial possibilities,
that Anselm now wishes "*sciens grammaticam*" to be interpreted,
i.e. as "Cl⟨trm$<\gamma>$⟩". Once this is realised, then the thesis,
"*grammaticus est sciens grammaticam*" may be seen as an assertion
having the higher-order "ε" as its main functor, as opposed to the
functor of the same semantical category as the lower-order "ε"
which its closeness in outward form to "*Omne sciens grammaticam
est grammaticum*" might appear to indicate. In fact, "*sciens grammaticam*" is at this point approaching "*scire grammaticam*" in sense.
The most striking support, however, for the suggestions which are
now being made comes from Anselm's discussion of a sentence
which runs parallel to "*grammaticus est sciens grammaticam*",

namely, *"albus est habens albedinem"*. Anselm goes to very great lengths in order to show that, given the logical context, *"habens albedinem"* as it occurs in this statement signifies neither *aliquid habens albedinem* nor *qui habet albedinem*. An interpretation which would agree with Anselm's arguments at this point is as

.1 $Cl\{w\} \varepsilon Cl\{trm<\omega>\}$

Under this interpretation neither the *"albus"* nor the *"habens albedinem"* of *"albus est habens albedinem"* are names; they are functors (verbs, predicates). Anselm's refusal (at 4.81) to allow *"habens albedinem"*, in this context, to become either *"aliquid habens albedinem"* or *"qui habet albedinem"* may thus be seen as a refusal to allow *"habens albedinem"* to have that reference which it would have, were it being used as a name. This is an illustration on his part of how logical statements, even if they do not, like *"grammaticus est grammatica"*, go shockingly beyond the bounds of ordinary grammatical classification, nevertheless need not take on the first and most obvious interpretation which ordinary grammar would allow. Anselm's argument at this point might have been specially designed to go clean against Priscian's equation of *"faciens eloquentem"* with *"qui facit eloquentem"* (*KIII* 160.13) mentioned above, and after the pattern of which *"albus est (idem quod) habens albedinem"* would indeed have had to be interpreted as:

.2 $[a] : a \varepsilon w . \equiv . a \varepsilon trm<\omega>$

Further, Anselm's own statement of what his sense of *"albus est idem quod habens albedinem"* is *not* concerned to embrace (and yet which it does not of course eliminate as an alternative in *usus loquendi*) aims at rejecting lower-order functors of the sort which appear in .2. For when he says, *"Non agitur utrum omnis qui est albus sit aliquid aut sit qui habet"* (4.810) he is at least saying that the following is indeed true:

.3 $[a] : a \varepsilon w . \supset . ob(a)$

but that this is not in question here. He continues with examples of his point, expressed in *de re* and *de voce* styles: *sed utrum hoc nomen sua significatione contineat hoc quod dicitur aliquid aut qui habet—sicut homo continet animal—ut quomodo homo est animal rationale mortale, ita albus sit aliquid habens albedinem* (4.810). It may be noted that the *"continet"* of this assertion (like the *"constat"* of 4.240) and the *"est"* of *"homo est animal rationale mortale"* are plainly interpretable in terms of the high-order *"ε"*. Thus, *"homo continet animal"* has the form:

.4 $\text{Cl}\{h\}\ \varepsilon \subset \{a\}$

and *"homo est animal rationale mortale"* has the form:

.5 $\text{Cl}\{h\}\ \varepsilon\ \text{Cl}\{a \cap r \cap m\}.$

§6.3127 Taking the text as a whole, therefore, with its parallel cases, and without having to assume that functors such as *"continet"*, *"constat"*, and the various relevant occurrences of *"est"* are mere metaphors veiling what are really *de voce* assertions (an assumption which would be contrary to Anselm's *de voce/de re* distinction (4.601–4.603)), there would appear to be no reason why the *"sciens grammaticam"* which is inferred at 4.31 should not have the logical status of "$\text{Cl}\{\text{trm}\langle\gamma\rangle\}$"—a logical status which Priscian's doctrine of participles already appears to suggest as a possibility.

§6.3128 *Sciens grammaticam*, understood as suggested in the last paragraph, is Anselm's definition of a specimen paronym, the applicability of which is accidental, not essential, to the being of an object. From the remarks made by the Tutor at 4.24121, it looks as though Anselm is not recognizing anything corresponding to Aquinas' distinction between *accidentia individui* and *propriae passiones vel generis vel speciei* (*ADEE* 7). However, both Anselm and Aquinas agree that *ex accidente et subiecto non fit unum per se; unde non resultat ex eorum coniunctione aliqua natura cui intentio generis vel speciei possit attribui* (*ADEE* 7, cf. 4.2411). Anselm's present solution is not only entirely in accordance with the spirit of Aquinas' general statement, just quoted, but also fulfills the various requirements which the definition of an accident must fulfill, e.g. askability of the *"alterum aliquid"* question, and the absence of necessity for redefinition on extension of application (cf. §5.410).

§6.3129 It has been shown that *"habens* (or *sciens*) *grammaticam"* and *"habens albedinem"* in the definitional context of the dialogue are verbal (as opposed to nominal) in nature, i.e. they are there to be interpreted as instances of "Cl⟨trm<γ>⟩". However, it is also plain that in such contexts *"habens* α", where "α" is an abstract noun, can be equated with "α" itself; this is shown by 4.31, 4.4233, 4.801, and 4.712, and by the way, traced above, in which *grammaticus est grammatica* (or *"grammaticus" significat grammaticam"*) has figured as an alternative to *grammaticus est sciens grammaticam* (or *"grammaticus" significat scientem grammaticam*). In order, therefore, to give an indication of the sense of these abstract nouns in such contexts (as opposed to those in which they are name-forming) use will be made of definition §6.22.17, thus yielding the counterpart of the equivalence here plainly presupposed by Anselm, yet at the same time maintaining the notational distinction observed by him; i.e. *"grammatica"* as it occurs in *"grammaticus est grammatica"* can be construed as "Cl⟨γ⟩" which is equivalent to "Cl⟨trm<γ>⟩ (*"sciens* (or *habens*) *grammaticam"*). This convention will be found to cohere with the interpretations of definitional presuppositions now to be suggested.

§6.32   *Presuppositions concerning definition and theory*

§6.321   To define, says Anselm (3.800) is to give the *esse* of a thing; in so saying he echoes Boethius' words (*BCP*129D, *BDT*-1196C). Already, in view of the earlier discussions of the semantical status of Anselm's assertions regarding *esse* it is clear that an inspection of his definitional presuppositions will involve recourse to an "ε" having functorial arguments (§6.3111).

§6.322   The general ancient concern that definitions should reflect states of affairs, and yet at the same time not suffer the fluctuations to which states of affairs are subject has been suggested as one of the roots of the dialogue, and as the basis of the distinction between substance-theories (with their definitions) and non-substance ("accident") theories (with their special problems of definition the

solution of which is one of the concerns of the dialogue) (§5.1).
Intra-theoretical ("substantial") predications were said to be "*de
subiceto*"; extra-theoretical ("accidental") predictions were said
to be of things "*in subiecto*" (*BC*169-196). Intra-theoretical predications are of two sorts, namely, *in eo quod quid* (possible responses
to the question "*Quid sit?*") and *in eo quod quale* (possible responses to the question "*Quale sit?*") (*BDP*26C-D, *BDF*892D-
893A); not all *in eo quod quale* predications, however, are *de
subiecto*. Nevertheless, when definition is carried out by means
of *genus* and *differentia* (as when *man* is defined as *rational animal*), "animal" (*genus*) is here said to be predicated *in eo quod quid*
and "rational" (*differentia*) is predicated *in eo quod quale*, and
both predications are in this case *de subiecto*, i.e. intra-theoretical.
Since an investigation of Boethius' notion of *genus, species, differentia*, and the other predicables would require a separate work, the
most economical fashion of coming to terms with these notions for
the purpose of the present study will be to assume that definitions
in respect of substance-theories are in question, and to introduce
genus (Γ) and *differentia* (△) as undefined constant terms; these
can then be used for the elucidation of the notion of species (of substance) (E), thus:

.1   [*a*] : Cl⟨*a*⟩ ε E . ≡ . ex(*a*) . [∃ *b*φ] . Cl⟨*b*) ε Γ .
             Cl⟨φ⟩ ε △ . Cl⟨*a*⟩ ε Cl⟨*b* ∩ trm<φ>⟩

(See definitions .1, .11, .14, .15, .17, and .22 of §6.22 in respect of
the functors here exploited). This elucidation is pitched at the
level of the higher-order "ε" in view of the reminder given above
that definition (of which the notions of *genus, species*, and *differentia*, are the instruments) concerns the *esse* of the definiendum,
and hence must be pitched at this higher level (§6.311). Again,
before the present study was undertaken, C. Lejewski had already
shown that sentences such as "*man* is a species" should be analysed
at such a level (*LA*247-249). It should therefore be evident that
the terms "Γ", "E", and "△" are verbal or functorial in nature,
and should hence, strictly speaking, be read off as (for example)
"forming a *genus*", "forming a *species*", and "constituting a *differ-*

entia" respectively. The existence-clause "ex(a)" has been included in the right-hand side of .1 in view of the demand which appears to have been made by Boethius and Aquinas that there should exist instances of the beings defined by substance-theories (*BTC*1092C, *APA*465, 466-467).

§6.323   Boethius and Anselm plainly believe that there are, as it were, lower limits to specificity (in the strict sense of "species") (4.2411); to regard certain species as generic in respect of their various sub-divisions (e.g., to regard literates as forming a sub-species of *man*) was for them to fall below the limits at which theories represent the world as we find it. Since no one would be inclined, at the pre-theoretical stage, to regard the pale and the blushing Socrates as two distinct objects, one of which comes into existence as the other perishes, it was therefore assumed that distinct theories of pale men and pink men are not called for. Again, to attach the theory of paleness to anthropology would be most uneconomical, since separate theories for other species of pale objects would be called for. In other words, there are *species specialissimae* (the *species* covered by §6.322.1 must be assumed to be such) and these are not to be posited at any arbitrary point in a descending scale of classification, but only at the point where an ultra-empiricism, utterly unlike the sophistications of the "empiricists" of the modern period, and leaving everything exactly as it is before the intervention of alternative theoretical descriptions, finds it. Again, *species specialissimae* are not to be identified, in the Leibnizian manner, on the model of Aquinate angelology, with individuals.

§6.324   A conception of "object" is hence here in question which represents a restriction on the more general notion made available in Ontology: thus, "that of which there is exactly one" might be said to be the Ontological picture of "object", as is evidenced by the definition:

.1 $[a] : \mathrm{ob}(a) \ . \ \equiv \ . \ [\exists b] \ . \ a \ \varepsilon \ b$ (§6.22.3, *LR* T16)

(The *definiendum* may here be read off as "There exists exactly one

a" or "a is an object"). This definition allows the very widest latitude in the choice of objects; thus any space-time segment of the physical world, no matter how fancifully selected, as well as purely notional constructs such as spatio-temporal minimals may count as objects according to .1. Conversely, looking at the matter from the point of view of a's *non-* objecthood, there is no name (apart, of course, from "a" itself, and "$\vee$" (defined §6.22.18)) which if denied of a would amount to denial of its existing objecthood. Anselm's remarks on specificity (4.2411) make it plain that neither he nor Boethius, from whom the vocabulary of these remarks is directly drawn, are working with the very general notion of "object" which is provided by Ontology, but rather on a restriction or particularisation of that notion; the reason for this is quite plain: they are accustomed to work in terms not of Ontology, but of the theories of those particular types of objects (men, animals, rocks, plants, etc.) which lie within the field of their ultra-empiricism in this respect. Within such theories, or within the fragmentary sketches of such theories, theses involving non-Ontological constant terms are available according to which denial of certain predicates amounts to the denial of the existence of an object of the sort comprehended by the theory in question. For example, it follows from the theses of anthropology which the ancients made explicit that to say of a particular man that he is not an animal is to say that he does not exist. Conversely, it is only to the extent that such predicates are true of him that that man is an object subsumable under the terms deployed in anthropology. What we have here, then, is not so much an abrogation of Ontology, the most general theory of objects, as a set of limitations imposed for the purposes of theories of a particular range of sorts of object: the truth of the theses of Ontology is not impugned—thus "Socrates" still lies within the substitution-range of the universal quantifier in .1 above—for these other theories, even though one may be able to clothe them in the language of Ontology, as is attempted in the present work, are not Ontology, in virtue of their involving or presupposing constant terms which do not belong to Ontology. Alternatively, one may state the position thus: it is plain from their use of "*unum aliquid*" (cf. 4.2414, 4.72) that Anselm and his predecessors, working in terms of "natural" language, were haunted by the fear that, given an unlimited substitution-range in name-quantification, they might find themselves committed, e.g. by equivocal names, to a break-down of the universality of certain logical principles such as that of the excluded middle. It is their desire for concretely-guided qualification in this matter of what is to count as being an object, and hence also, as being named by a "safe" name, which separates them off from modern logicians who develop quantificational theory without explicit restrictions on object-hood of the sort described. In a fashion, both the meeting-point and the parting of the ways between ancient and modern logic, and perhaps between Aristotelian metaphysics and certain forms of modern logic, lies just in their field of the discussion of quantifier-ranges. The ancients sacrificed generality in order to retain recognisable objects: some moderns gain generality at the price of emptying their systems of anything recognisably approaching empirical object-hood and lack the capacity for any re-introduction of the latter—a lack which is not found, however, in the systems of S. Leśniewski.

§6.325   The limitations on the scope of object-hood which have been mentioned above could be given a simple logical representation by imposing appropriate restrictions on the range of quantifiers used in theory-exposition. Thus it would be possible to assemble theses of anthropology in which the range of substitutions for nominal variables would be limited to the proper names of human beings; the variables bound by such quantification would then no longer be akin to colourless impersonal pronouns, but would carry with them the tinge of personal pronouns which had reference. Under such circumstances, to say "For some he (or she)—he (or she) is not a human being" would amount to the denial of the existence of some person, thereby reproducing that *corruptio subiecti* which the theory of definition presupposed by Anselm demands should follow in such a case (4.2411).

§6.33   *Analysis of the Course of the Argument*

§6.331   In spite of Prantl's remark that *De grammatico* has a wandering quality, it will in fact be found that its dialectical structure lends it an elegant symmetry which can still be exploited for expository purposes in connection with the analyses now to be suggested. Thus the thesis of the dialogue is to be found in the theoretical assertions concerning *literate* listed as Th7-Th17 below, with *grammaticus est grammatica* as its scandalous core. The antithesis is based on *usus loquendi* and matters of lower-order fact, and expresses itself in the form of uneasiness at the apparent incompatibility between these and the theoretical assertions mentioned. The reconciliation between thesis and antithesis lies in the distinction between precisive and oblique signification (4.232); the first of these does justice to the technical requirements of definition, while the second takes account of the claims of *usus loquendi*. There now follows a list of some of the main features of the thesis, antithesis, and facts reflected in *usus loquendi*. Those which are expressed in *de re* fashion are for the most part accompanied by a suggested analysis in terms of the language of Ontology as described and discussed above. The numeration of this material is effected in such a way that reference can be made to it in the survey of the main course of the dialogue which is presented in §6.335.

§6.332   *Thesis*

There now follow elements of the thesis, expressed in terms of the exemplary non-paronymous (substance) names "man" and "stone" and of the the exemplary paronyms "literate" and "white". Sufficient theses have been assembled to form a basis for following the course of the dialogue in §6.335, but no claim is made that the following exhaust the presuppositions of the work. References to relevant definitions and discussions are given after each analysis in terms of Ontology which are hereunder suggested.

Th1 *Man* is a species (of sub-   (1.12, 4.1104, 4.231, 4.2411)
    stance)   (§6.22.14, §6.22.15, §6.322.1)

      Cl $\{$h$\}$ ε E

Th2 *Man* is *rational* (*mortal*)   (3.21, 3.8010, 4.240)
    animal   (§6.22.11, §6.22.14, §6.22.15, §6.22.21)

Cl⟨h⟩ ε Cl⟨a ⌢ trm<λ>⟩

(The "mortal" part of the definition of *man* used by Anselm will be ignored; it was employed by Boethius on grounds derived from speculative astronomy (*BCP*93A, 127B, *BTC*1070C-D, 1101D)).

Th3   *Animal* is a genus   (3.8010, 4.240)
      Cl⟨a⟩ ε Γ   (§6.22.14, §6.22.15, §6.322.1)

Th4   *Rationality* is a *differentia*   (3.511, 3.8010, 4.240)
      Cl⟨λ⟩ ε △   (§6.22.15, §6.22.17, §6.322.1, §6.3129)

Th5   *Man* is a species (of substance) having *animal* as its genus and rationality as its differentia   (3.8010)
      Cl⟨h⟩ ε E . ≡ . ex (h) . Cl⟨a⟩ ε Γ . Cl⟨λ⟩ ε △ .
               Cl⟨h⟩ ε Cl⟨a ⌢ trm<λ>⟩   (§6.322.1

Th6   "Man" signifies substance   (Th1, 4.231)

Th7   Every man can be understood without literacy   (3.102, Th5)

Th8   Every man can be understood to be (a) man without literacy   (3.311, Th7)
      ~ (Cl⟨h⟩ ε Cl ⟨trm<γ>⟩)   (§6.22.11, §6.22.14, §6.22.15
                             §6.3114)

Th9   *Literate* is literacy   (4.232, 4.2341, 4.31, 4.5022)
      Cl⟨g⟩ ε Cl⟨γ⟩   (§6.22.14, §6.22.15, §6.22.17, §6.3129)

Th10 "Literate" signifies literacy precisively (*per se*)   (4.232,4.31)

Th11 "Literate" signifies *having literacy* (precisively)   (4.31)

Th12 *Literate* is a quality   (1.201, 4.610, cf. Th9)

Th13 "Literate" signifies a quality   (4.602. cf. Th12)

Th14 *White* is *having whiteness*   (4.801)
      Cl⟨w⟩ ε Cl⟨trm<ω>⟩   (§6.22.11, §6.22.14, §6.22.15)

Th15 "White" is equisignificant with "having whiteness" (4.4233, 4.801)

Th16 No literate can be understood without literacy (3.101; cf. Th9, Th10

Th17 No literate can be understood to be literate without literacy
$$(3.312, Th16)$$

$$Cl\{g\} \ \varepsilon \ Cl\{trm<\gamma>\} \qquad (\S6.22.11, \ \S6.22.14, \ \S6.22.15,$$
$$\S6.3114)$$

Th18 Being a man does not demand literacy $(3.41 \ (=Th8) \ )$
$$\sim \ (Cl\{h\} \ \varepsilon \ Cl\{trm<\gamma>\}) \qquad (\S6.22.11, \ \S6.22.14, \ \S6.22.15)$$

Th19 Being literate demands literacy $(3.42 \ (=Th17))$
$$\sim \ (Cl\{h\} \ \varepsilon \ Cl\{trm<\gamma>\}) \qquad (\S6.22.11, \ \S6.22.14, \ \S6.22.15)$$
$$\S6.3114)$$

Th20 Being literate is not being man $(3.431, from Th18, Th19)$
$$\sim \ (Cl\{g\} \ \varepsilon \ Cl\{h\}) \qquad (\S6.22.14, \ \S6.22.15, \ \S6.3111)$$

Th21 *Literate* and *man* are not identically defined $(3.44, Th20)$
$$\sim \ (Cl\{g\} \ = \ Cl\{h\}) \qquad (\S6.22.14, \ \S6.22.16)$$

Th22 No man is in some sense understandable without rationality
$$(3.6321, Th5)$$

Th23 Every stone is in any sense understandable without rationality (3.6322)

Th24 No stone is in any sense a man $(3.63221, Th22, Th23)$

Th25 Everything which is literate can be understood to be (a) man
without literacy (3.6333, Th5, Th9, and perhaps UI (below))

Th26 No man can be understood to be literate without literacy
$$(3.6334)$$

Th27 Being white is not being a man $(3.9411, cf. 4.24121)$
$$\sim \ (Cl\{w\} \ \varepsilon \ Cl\{h\}) \qquad (\S6.22.14, \ \S6.22.15, \ \S6.3111)$$

Th28 Being literate is compatible with being a non-man
$$(3.9421, cf. 4.2412)$$

Th29 "Literate" signifies man only obliquely (*per aliud*) (4.232,
cf. U4 below))

Th30 "Literate" is appellative of man $(4.233; cf. Th29)$

Th31 "Literate" does not signify man precisively (4.233)

Th32 "Literate" is not appellative of literacy (4.234; cf. U3 below)

§6.333 Truths external to the theories of exemplary paronyms "literate" and "white" (4.430, 4.515), which are reflected in *usus loquendi*, and which constitute the main basis of the antithesis (cf. §6.334):

U1 All literates are men   (1.11)
    $g \subset h$ (§6.22.4)

U2 "Literate" is not used to refer to men without literacy (4.240)

U3 "Literate" is not used to refer to literacy (4.20, 4.21; contrast Th9, Th10)

U4 "Literate" is used to refer to men   (4.21)

U5 [A] white is a haver of whiteness   (4.810)

U6 [A] white is something having whiteness   (4.810)

U7 Some whites are non-men   (3.9412, 4.24121)
    $w \triangle \sim h$ (§6.22.6, §6.22.22)

§6.334 *Antithesis*

The elements of the antithesis now follow; these are, for the most part, drawn from the extra-theoretical truths listed in the last paragraph.

A1 [A] literate is [a] man having literacy   (U1, 4.240)
    $g \circ h \cap trm{<}\gamma{>}$ (§6.22.9, §6.22.11, §6.22.20)

A2 "Literate" signifies *man* and literacy   (4.240; cf. A1)

A3 *Literate* is a substance   (U1, A1)

A4 "Literate" signifies substance   (A2)

A5 *Literate* is a species having *man* as its genus and literacy as its *differentia*   (4.2411, A2)
$$Cl\{g\} \; \varepsilon \; E \; . \; \equiv \; . \; ex(g) \; . \; Cl\{h\} \; \varepsilon \; \Gamma \; . \; Cl\{\gamma\} \; \varepsilon \; \triangle \; .$$
$$Cl\{g\} \; \varepsilon \; Cl\{h \cap trm{<}\gamma{>}\}   (§6.322.1)$$

§6.335   Hence, ignoring certain subsidiary arguments which arise in connection with the Student's objections, the main course of the dialogue may be outlined as follows:

1.000–2.00: The apparently opposed alternatives *"Literate* is substance" (A3) and *"Literate* is quality" (Th12) are mooted, and *prima facie* reasons for both of them are offered. Thus the first alternative seems to be supported by the fact that all literates are men (U1), whereas the technical verdict of the philosophers supports the second (Th12). The Tutor hints that one can find senses in which both alternatives are true—a reference to the distinctions which will be presented at 4.23.

3.00–3.452: "No literate is man" (3.113) apparently follows from a first set of technical theses, i.e. from Th7 and Th16; a primary analysis of the latter (Th8 and Th17) blocks the inference (3.31), and a further analysis (Th18, Th19) shows that the weaker thesis "Being literate is not being a man" (Th20) and its corresponding definitional statement (Th21) are the true conclusions from Th7 and Th16, thus ultimately analysed.

3.500–3.543 represent the Student's mistaken response to a test question.

3.60–3.6341 contrast the case of *stone* and *man* with that of *man* and *literate*. It can be established, by a syllogism of the same form as that of 3.11, as well as by a stronger, internally quantified version of it, that:

.1 No stone is in any sense a man   (3.62, 3.63221) which might be analysed as

.2 $[x] . \sim (x \, \varepsilon \, 1 . \equiv . x \, \varepsilon \, h)$

However, one cannot come to a like conclusion regarding *man* and *literate* by producing a similarly internally quantified version of 3.11 itself, i.e. one cannot assert:

.3 No literate is in some sense understandable without literacy
(3.6331, cf. 3.101)

.4 Every man is in any sense understandable without literacy
(3.6332, cf. 3.102)

which, if true, would allow us to conclude, in a fashion similar to that exemplified in the case of *man* and *stone* that

.5 No literate is in any sense a man (3.6341)

i.e.

.6 $[x]$. $\sim$ $(x \, \varepsilon \, g$. $\equiv$. $x \, \varepsilon \,$ h

For, contrary to .3 and .4 respectively, we have the following truths, from which .5 cannot be inferred:

.7 Everything which is literate can be understood to be a man without literacy (3.6333)

.8 No man can be understood to be a literate without literacy (3.6334)

These premisses, it may be noted, are identical with those produced at 3.11, 3.12 (Th7 and Th17 respectively), except that the first occurrences of "man" and "literate" in the two latter have been interchanged. Up to the point of this interchange, therefore, the premisses have been part of the thesis; however, the interchange itself is based on the extra-theoretical fact (U1) that every literate *is* a man; and U1 in its turn is the basis of the signification statement designed to do justice to the extra-theoretical facts reflected in *usus loquendi*, viz: "literate" signifies *man* obliquely (Th29), is appellative of *man* (Th30) (4.232–4.2341).

3.700–3.921 are occupied with the statement and refutation of a sophism of the Student's (3.700–3.7211) which attempts to draw an antifactual conclusion (3.7211: No literate is a man) (contrast U1) from the theoretical conclusion 3.431 (Being literate is not being man) (Th20). After a refutation by means of a parallel argument giving an absurd conclusion (3.800–3.811), the sophism is resolved by the introduction of the qualification *"simpliciter"*, the effect of which is to bring out the fact that Th20 amounts to the negation of an identity (cf. the analysis suggested for Th21) rather than of an inclusion.

3.940–3.9431 contains a preliminary suggestion of the parity between the cases covered by Th27 and Th20, a parity which is later confirmed (4.24121).

4.100–4.112: At 4.10 the Student again tries to draw the same anti-factual conclusion (No literate is a man) from further theoretical statements. In reply (4.110–4.112) the Tutor gives a first indication of what his solution to the problem as formulated at the opening of the dialogue (i.e. the opposition of Th12 and A3 (or Th13 or A4)) will be: "Literate" (in some as yet unspecified senses of "signify") signifies both *man* and *literate,* i.e. can be said to "be" both substance and quality.

4.1200–4.22: The Student opposes the substantiality of *literate* by correctly appealing to theoretical truths concerning *literate* which bar this verdict (4.1200–4.122); in reply, the Tutor rather treacherously appeals to the theoretical features of the *reference* of "literate", i.e. he bases himself on U4, which is not itself strictly part of the theory of "literate", although account is ultimately taken of U4 in Th29 and Th30 (4.130–4.132). The suspicion that the Tutor is deliberately tying his interlocutor in knots is expressed by the Student in 4.14; the latter then again attempts to demolish the logicians' technical verdict on *literate,* this time not by attempting to show that their theses have anti-factual conclusions, but by drawing a direct contrast between logicians' assertions and *usus loquendi* (4.21; cf. A3, A4, U4, as opposed to Th10–Th13). As a way out of this difficulty the Student puts forward what may be called the Priscian-Mill thesis (§4.3131) according to which "literate" and like names signify in the same way as "man" and its fellow substance-names (4.22): this is in fact an extension to the case of substance-names of the verdict already reached at 4.111 and 4.112, namely, that *literate* (in some unspecified senses of "signify") signifies *both* substance and quality.

4.230–4.2341. In reply, the Tutor gives his version of the difference between substance-terms and other names which has been outlined in §5.2, in particular, he calls attention to the unity and completive nature of substances (4.231). Given the explanations which accompany the definitions of the forms of expression which are involved in Th5, one might say that Th5 is here being defended and opposed to e.g. A5, which is false, for example, because literacy is not a *differentia* in respect of substance; it cannot be used as a *differentia* to create a sub-species of *man* because, for instance, Th25 is true. Then come the distinctions which clear up the senses of "signify" lying behind some of the previous confusion; there is that sense of "signify" which represents the intra-theoretical aspects of a term, signification in its precisive, proper, sense; it is only in this sense that "literate" can be said to signify literacy (Th10). However, as a matter of fact which is, strictly speaking, extra-theoretical in respect of *literate,* the word "literate" can be said to signify *man* obliquely (Th29); this is because in *usus loquendi* it is used to refer to human beings (U4); it is, as Anselm puts it, hence *appellative* of human beings (Th30). "Literate" is not, however, appellative of literacy (Th32, cf. U3), nor is it precisively significative of *man* (Th31). All this accounts for the *de voce* side of the matter (cf. 4.602). Thus we now have an accord between *usus loquendi* and the oblique signification of a paronym: "The literate is a man" makes good sense. Yet when the *de re* correlate of the paronym's precisive signification is stated (as in *"Literate* is literacy" (Th9)) there is then no such accord (4.232–4.2341).

4.240–4.31. Nevertheless, the Student continues to uphold the Priscian-Mill thesis of 4.22 to the effect that "man" and "literate" signify in the same way. He backs up his contention by a continued appeal to *usus loquendi:* he reminds the Tutor of what in fact is the *reference* of "literate"; the Student's definition of *literate* is hence *man displaying literacy* (4.240, cf. A1 and U1). This amounts to accepting A5, i.e. *literate* is a species of the genus *man,* literacy being the *differentia,* with all its attendant absurdities from the pretheoretical viewpoint, e.g. we will find ourselves having to say that a new entity has come into existence in those situations where ordinarily we would just say that a man has *become* literate (4.2411). Again, a difficulty urged in our own time by A. Church (*CR*) arises in connection with the supposable (i.e. possible) situation wherein "literate" applies to some rational being other than a man (Th28); in the Tutor's terms, the Student's contention makes possible the contradictory statement that some non-man (i.e. the non-human literate) is a man (according to the Student's definition) (4.-2412). The correct definition of "literate" should therefore leave open the reference of the term, just as a definition of "white" should (4.24-121). Again, inclusion of "man" in the definition of "literate" would make the "man" of "literate man" superfluous, which it is not (4.2413). An infinite regress is entailed, if the Student's definition is accepted

(4.2414). Finally, to include the reference of a paronym in the paronym's definition would, the Tutor claims, have unfortunate repercussions in connection with the grammarian's definition of a verb (4.2414). *Man* must therefore be excluded from the Student's proposal, leaving only *displaying literacy* (*sciens grammaticam*) as the definition sought (Th11). And it is in this sense, concludes the Tutor, that "literate" can be said to signify literacy (4.3, Th10).

4.40–4.431. The way in which, in concrete circumstances, the reference of a paronym—a reference whose full statement would involve the use of a substance-name—fills out the incompleteness of the precisive signification of a paronym, is illustrated by means of the case of "white"; here the precisive signification is merely "having whiteness" (4.4233, Th15) and in the absence of contextual or habitual supplementation the use of "white" as a name hence leaves the hearer unsatisfied as regards the reference intended; the use of the senses or an anticipation generated by repeated sense-experience can provide the requisite supplementation, but the latter is not part of the precisive signification of the paronym (4.40–4.4242). Further, the distinction between precisive and oblique signification extends also to verbs (4.4243); this extension constitutes the main connecting link between *De grammatico* and almost all of Anselm's other writings; in these, as I have tried to show in *HG,* the distinction is exploited for the purpose of sentential analysis of that sort for which the programme is laid down in *SNUW.* For further information on St. Anselm's logic outside *De grammatico,* see *HL, HM, HN, HP.*

4.500–4.611: The Student's continuing qualms on the verdict thus agreed represent his lingering doubts about the break with *usus loquendi* to which he, as a logician, is now committed. Anyone who is still unconvinced that the strangeness of "*grammaticus* is a quality" (Th12) with its consequence "*grammaticus est grammatica*" (Th9) has been a stumbling block from the very opening sentence of the dialogue need only read 4.5 and 4.6, where the question is again overtly raised (4.501, 4.5022) to receive its final answer by reference to the practices of the grammarians themselves. In addition, we have a sophism which turns on the ambiguity of the Latin word "*solus*" propounded (4.5020, 4.5021, 4.503) and resolved by reference to the notion of an ordered series (4.503–4.5121). The remainder of these sections attempts to show that the notion of precisive signification accords with Aristotle's modes of expression as they occur in the *Categoriae* (4.513–4.515) and makes explicit the distinction between assertions *de voce* and assertions *de re* which has, in effect, been taken for granted in the dialogue up to the present point (4.60-4.61): given this distinction, and given Aristotle's disregard of it at times (4.604), the conclusion that *literate* is a quality (Th12) may, declares the Tutor, be interpreted in either sense.

4.620–4.621: The scandal of the discord between *usus loquendi* and the assertions of logicians, a scandal which was still disturbing the Student at 4.5022, is here finally resolved by a reminder of the parallel case from grammatical writings: no one would take technical grammatical assertions such as "*lapis* is masculine" to have repercussions in ordinary discourse (e.g. one would not thence conclude that a stone is a masculine object); the same applies to technical logical assertions.

4.600–4.72:   Possible variations in the technical verdict, insofar as the category to which *literate* is assigned might be questioned, are next discussed (4.700), and in consequence a further contrast drawn between the way in which paronyms signify and that in which substance-words signify (4.71). 4.72 contains an elucidation of the phrase "forming a single whole" which occurred in the course of the contrast mentioned; here the Tutor specifies the sorts of theoretical descriptions he would be prepared to give of what may, in view of the points made in §5.2, be called "unambiguously-countables" (cf. *AG3P86*)

4.800–4.83: The closing section of the dialogue is most valuable insofar as it elucidates the semantical categories involved in assertions such as "*Literate* is literacy" (Th9), "*White* is *having whiteness*" (Th14) (and hence in "*Literate* is *displaying literacy*" which is the *de re* correlate of one of the conclusions reached in 4.31). Thus the Student suggests (4.80) that the arguments of the "is" of the sentences just quoted are nominal in nature (e.g. Th14 should be interpreted as "Something white is something having white-ness") as opposed to functorial, predicative, or verbal. Interspersed with this suggestion is a sophistical disjunctive syllogism which will receive separate treatment in §6.342 below. That the arguments of sentences such as Th14 should, however, be functorial rather than nominal appears to be the burden of the Tutor's counter-contention: he urges that although the Student's analysis does not yield a falsehood, yet that analysis is beside the point in relation to the matter in hand, i.e. the determination of the precisive signifi-cation of "white" (and its fellow paronyms) (4.810–4.811). This contention is underpinned by a demonstration of the regresses to which the Student's analysis leads; these are avoided if that analysis is resisted. (For a discussion in detail of these regresses, see §6.341 below). The Student's sophisms are resolved (4.813), the dialogue's conclusions generalised (4.82), and their provisional nature stressed (4.83).

§6.34   *Some subsidiary arguments*

§6.341   *The final regresses*

§6.3411 Throughout the foregoing analysis, part of the opposition between Tutor and Students has been represented as a disagree-ment as to the semantical status of the definitional sentences which constitute part of their discourse. I have suggested that the Student thinks of such sentences as having nominal arguments, but that the Tutor sees these arguments as verbal (i.e. predicative, or functorial) in nature. A confirmation that this really is the sort of disagreement which is in question appears to be provided when, at 4.801, the ques-tion is raised as to how

.1   *Albus est (idem quod) habens albedinem*

(which both Student and Tutor are prepared to assert) is to be interpreted. The Student opts for an interpretation of .1 such that the arguments of its "*est (idem quod)*" are supposed to be unavoidably nominal; forthwith the Tutor rejoins that such an interpretation, though not giving rise to falsehood, is nevertheless irrelevant to the present context, and shows that it leads to an infinite regress which his own (non-nominal) interpretation avoids; this he construes as evidence for the rejection of the Student's interpretation. Details of this regress and its avoidance now follow. The literary variants of "*est (idem quod)*" which occur in the text (i.e. "*non est aliud quam*", "*recte semper accipitur pro*" etc.) and their *de voce* alternatives (e.g. "*significat*") are hereunder replaced by "o", the sign of weak identity (cf. §6.22).

§6.3412 The Student gives of §6.3411.1 the following interpretation (4.801):

.1 *albus* o *aliquid habens albedinem*

which is intended to bring out the nominal nature of the arguments of "o", i.e. is of the form:

.2 $\text{w} \circ \text{trm} < \omega >$

He then accepts (4.8120):

.3 *aliquid habens albedinem* o *aliquid album*

i.e.

.4 $\text{trm} < \omega > \circ \text{trm} < \varepsilon \{\text{w}\} >$

then from identities .1 and .3 he finds himself committed to the following further identity:

5. *albus* o *aliquid album*

i.e.

.6 $\text{w} \circ \text{trm} < \varepsilon \{\text{w}\} >$

Given the fact that throughout the discussion it has been made plain that the gender of "*albus*" is here immaterial, the identity given in .5 can plainly be used to effect substitutions of "*aliquid album*" wherever "*albus*" or "*album*" appear, so that from .5 itself one can infer:

.7 *aliquid album* o *aliquid aliquid album*

In other terms, one has, from .6:

.8 $\text{trm} < \varepsilon \{\text{w}\} > \circ \text{trm} < \varepsilon \{\text{trm} < \varepsilon \{\text{w}\} > \} >$

And the regresses initiated in .7 and .8 can plainly, by .5 and .6 respectively, be continued to infinity. Thus, it is concluded, §6.3411.1 must be rejected as an interpretation of the agreed definition of *albus*. Anselm's intuition that the definition must remain at the level of functors having verbs, not names, as arguments, if regress is to be avoided, is now interpreted and confirmed. It may be further strengthened by the consideration that even the Student's regress-generating assertions (.1, .3, .5), if interpreted as having verbs, as opposed to names, as arguments of their "o", no longer give rise to regress. This change of level could be effected in the Latin by the device used elsewhere in the dialogue by Anselm, i.e. by placing *"esse"* before each of the names or nominal forms which occur as arguments in .1, .3, .5, and changing the case of each such name or nominal form into the genitive, e.g. *"esse albi"* would then be the first argument of .5. In the language of Ontology the corresponding sentences, i.e. .2, .4, and .6, would accordingly become:

.9 $Cl\{w\} \circ Cl\{trm<\omega>\}$

.10 $Cl\{trm<\omega>\} \circ Cl\{trm<\varepsilon\{w\}>\}$

.11 $Cl\{w\} \circ Cl\{trm<\varepsilon\{w\}>\}$

Here, while the counterpart of .6, i.e. .11, is still derivable from .9 and .10, nevertheless a regress cannot be generated by substitution of the first argument of the "o" of .11 for any part of the second argument which is equiform with that first argument, since there is now no such equiformity; a substitution of this sort was, however, made possible by .6. The proposed new Latin sentences would likewise be such as to avoid the regress, as may easily be verified. The possibility of a regress does therefore certainly reflect the use of a functor which in this definitional context is of an inappropriate semantical category, given Anselm's presuppositions on definition. Relatively to the resources of Ontology, however, the possibility of regress is of no logical significance, since .2, .4, and .6 are inferentially equivalent to .9, .10, and .11 respectively; given .11, therefore, inference of the regress from .6 is still possible.

§6.342   *The disjunctive sophism*

§6.3421 The sophistical argument of 4.8021 relies for its force on a supposed exemplification of the Principle of the excluded middle. It is assumed that *"albus aut aliquid significat habens albedinem aut nihil"* is such an exemplification, and from this it is concluded that since *nothing* cannot have whiteness, "white" must signify *something* having whiteness. The refutation given in 4.813 takes the form of a showing that this assumption does not represent the disjunction of a proposition and its negation, and hence is neither exhaustive of the situation (*non est integra*) nor true (*nec vera*). The reason given for this failure is that since "*nihil*" means "*non-aliquid*", an "infinite name" is being used as one member of the disjunction, with the result that the "*non*" prefixed to that name is confused with the "*non*" which should negate one of the alternants. The whole range of the possibilities of this kind of confusion is very fully treated in *De Interpretatione* and its commentaries, the chief texts in Boethius being *BDIL*342–354 and *BDIG*520–567; aspects of it are summarised in several other parts of the commentaries, notably *BDIL*363–4, *BDIG*447B, *BDIG*580B-D, and *BDIG*590B–591C. The particular instance in question here is that in which the predicate-term is negated instead of the verb, i.e. "*significat non aliquid*" is assumed by the Student to be the negation of "*significat aliquid*": Anselm's remarks when correcting the statement of the alternatives are in fact a reminder of what Boethius had to say; for example, "*est iustus homo*" and "*est non iustus homo*" are both affirmative forms, the latter having an infinite name (*non iustus*) as predicate; the true negation of "*est iustus homo*" is "*non est iustus homo*" (*BDIL*344–348, esp. 345B, 346B). Caietan's comment is that *haec est una oppositio, 'homo est iustus', 'homo non est iustus'; alia vero oppositio est, 'homo est non iustus', 'homo non est non iustus'. Non enim negatio fit nisi per oppositionem negativae particulae ad hoc verbum 'est', quod est nota praedicationis; APH*213: "*homo est non iustus*" is an "*affirmatio de infinito praedicato*" (*APH*217). Although the "*significat*" of the present text differs from all the examples mentioned in the quotations given, in that it is a verb other than "*est*", this does not affect the relevance of those examples since, as Boethius points out, forms such as "*homo ambulat*" have always equivalents such as "*homo ambulans est*" *BDIL*348C–349A).

§6.3422 The example of the blind man is aptly used by Anselm in order to illustrate the point at which the negation impinges when it is misplaced in a disjunction of the type described. The Student's argument relies on an interpretation such as that exemplified when "The blind man either sees something or nothing" is understood as, "The blind man either sees something or sees not-something"; this interpretation leaves the blind man seeing in the cases of both alternatives, when what are really required are one alternative in which he is said to see, and one in which he is said not to see, as in "The blind man either sees something or does not see something".

§6.3423 The systematic distinction described above, and so well-known to the ancients mentioned, appears to be unknown to Russell, who, when giving reasons why the Theory of Descriptions is necessary, uses "The present King of France is bald or not bald" as an alleged instance of the principle of the excluded middle; the correct doctrine is in effect rather belatedly imported as an *ad hoc* device (e.g. in *RI* Ch. XVI) under the rather misleading guise of the "primary and secondary occurrences of descriptions in propositions". Again, we find in this same chapter of Russell's locutions having exactly the same form as that of the Student's (4.8021) which is now undergoing criticism, e.g. "the description 'x' describes something or describes nothing" (*RI*170). This is associated with, and in the case of the first example, springs from, the author's insistence on "φx" as a basic logical form. With only this at his disposal, he has, for instance, to parse "'x is not a unicorn' is always true" as "'not-φx' is always true"; the former really (it would appear) involves the negation of the second argument of "is", i.e. is of the form "$x \ \varepsilon \sim b$", whereas the "not-φx" of the second conveys rather "$\sim (x \ \varepsilon \ b)$" (on the assumption that "φ" is "$\varepsilon\{b\}$"). In Ontology, however, with its axiomatic based on functors such as "ε", which have two names as arguments, the appropriate distinctions can be made at the outset, and do not have to be brought in under a strange form at a particular juncture when the need becomes desperate.

INDEX OF NAMES AND SUBJECTS

(Authors and works referred to are listed in §S0.13)